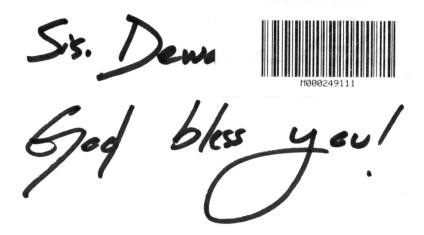

Sis. Dawn

God bless you!

Treasures of a Worshipper

A Collection of a Father's Wisdom and Daily Encouragement

James E. Tyson, II

Foreword by: J. LaVerne Tyson

Treasures of a Worshipper :

A Collection of a Father's Wisdom and Daily Encouragement

Copyright © 2017 by James E. Tyson, II,

Indianapolis, IN

For information contact :

James E. Tyson, II

www.jamestyson.org

Book and Cover design by Will Lewis, IV

ISBN : 978-0692903964

First Edition: August 2017

This book is dedicated to my son, Caden Shawn Tyson (aka Chief).

CONTENTS

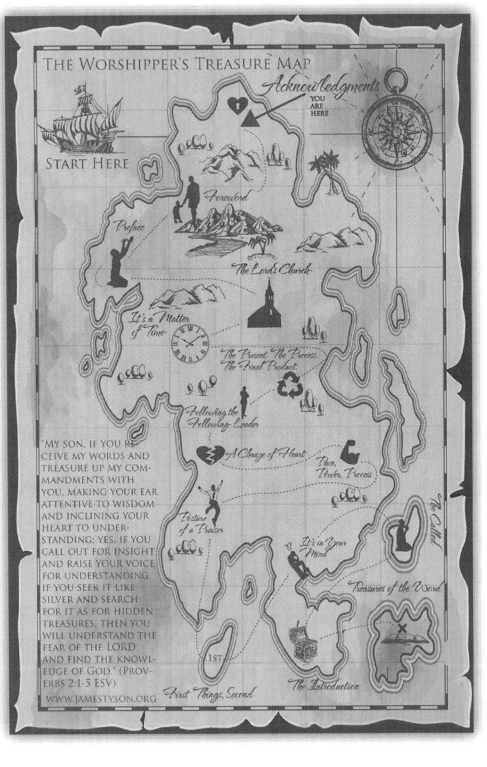

THE WORSHIPPER'S TREASURE MAP

Acknowledgments

YOU
ARE
HERE

START HERE

Foreword

Preface

The Lords Church

It's a Matter
of Time

The Present, The Process,
The Final Product.

Following the
Following Leader

A Change of Heart

Pain,
Power, Process

The Called

Posture
of a Praiser

It's in Your
Mind

Treasures of the Word

"MY SON, IF YOU RE
CEIVE MY WORDS AND
TREASURE UP MY COM-
MANDMENTS WITH
YOU, MAKING YOUR EAR
ATTENTIVE TO WISDOM
AND INCLINING YOUR
HEART TO UNDER-
STANDING; YES, IF YOU
CALL OUT FOR INSIGHT
AND RAISE YOUR VOICE
FOR UNDERSTANDING,
IF YOU SEEK IT LIKE
SILVER AND SEARCH
FOR IT AS FOR HIDDEN
TREASURES, THEN YOU
WILL UNDERSTAND THE
FEAR OF THE LORD
AND FIND THE KNOWL-
EDGE OF GOD." (PROV-
ERBS 2:1-5 ESV)

WWW.JAMESTYSON.ORG

1ST

First Things, Second

The Introduction

Acknowledgments

"IT'S NICE TO BE IMPORTANT, BUT IT'S MORE IMPORTANT TO BE NICE."- BISHOP JAMES E. TYSON

Growing up, I was taught to value others and the significant impact an individual has made in my life. This has been an amazing journey and there's no way I could have accomplished this on my own.

First, I thank God for the wonderful privilege of being used in His Kingdom. It is evident that worthiness has never been the concern of God; however, His choice takes precedent over an individual's feeling of worthiness. Because He chose my family and I, it causes me to be extremely humbled and grateful.

I'd also like to thank Heather Fox for assisting me in editing my book. I truly appreciate you. Among the editors, I appreciate my sister/administrator, Alecia White. Who would have thought the teenage boy you started working with over 10 years ago, you would be editing his book years later? Wow! Thank you for consistently supporting, being patient, and challenging me to accomplish this goal.

To my uncle, Bishop J. LaVerne Tyson, thank you for giving this young buck a chance. You consistently encouraged me during this process and you yielded your gift to help me accomplish my goal. Thank you, sir! Oh, and I'll remember you when I come into my Kingdom.

I would also like to thank my parents, Bishop C. Shawn and Lady Krista Tyson. There would be no James E., II without you. I am what I am because of you. I appreciate you never pressuring me to be you, but embrace who I am and excel. I love you both.

I celebrate the memory of one of heroes, the early (never late) Bishop James E. Tyson. I honor you and will forever appreciate the investment you deposited within me. I hope I'm making you proud.

Finally, I would like to thank my beautiful wife, Desiree, and my children, Caden and Kristen, for their patience and sacrifice. You'll be able to read this when you're older, but thanks, Chief and Kavey, for letting Daddy study and build this project during times that could have been spent with you. Desiree, thank you for being my wife and my strongest supporter. For every late night, road trip, and any open opportunity you let me read my manuscript or run an idea by you hundreds of times, thank you. Thank you for never belittling what was in me, but challenging me to be better. For every, "Try this" or "Fix that", thank you. Thank you for your strength and unwavering consistency. I love growing with you and I love you!

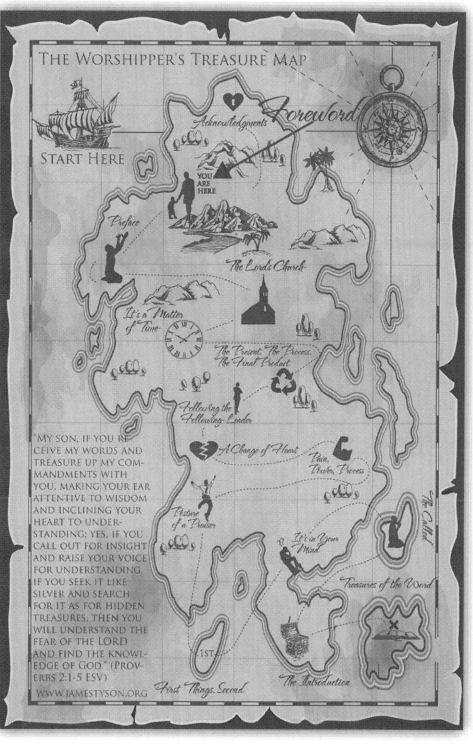

Foreword

"...QUALIS PATER TALIS FILIUS..."

About 36-37 years ago, I was a young, inexperienced pastor serving a very small congregation (about 20 people) in Warren, Ohio. In the 2-3 years since arriving at the fledgling church, I made decisions typical for a novice pastor trying to prove his worth. Many of my decisions ended up being catastrophic, and it wasn't long before I found myself fighting for my ministry life. I would often call my mother (Evelyn) and father (the late Bishop James E. Tyson) back home in Indianapolis for solace and an encouraging word. One such call led to my father telling me that my youngest brother, Shawn, had just preached his trial sermon. There had always been an exceptional anointing on my brother's young life, especially musically, but his anointing to preach didn't manifest itself until later in his teens.

I was anxious to hear "the kid" stumbling over his words and preaching for 4 minutes and 20 seconds like I did at my trial sermon! With that, my father told me he was going to send me a videotape of his sermon. A couple of weeks later the video arrived in the mail. That evening I sequestered myself in my "man cave" and watched my brother preaching his very first sermon. I was dumbfounded: BEYOND BELIEF!! I remember like it was yesterday thinking: "how could someone so young (I think my brother was 17 or 18 at the time) have the measure of depth and profoundness my brother exhibited on that tape?" His presentation, flow, and delivery was as if he had been preaching for 20 years! He had a "pulpit maturity" well beyond his years. As the proverbial saying goes, "the rest is history". Today, Bishop C. Shawn Tyson is one of Pentecost's most renowned pulpiters.

A couple of months ago, my nephew, Elder James Edison Tyson II (we call him "Jamie"), called me and asked if I would consider writing the foreword to his new book. I asked him what was the title and he answered, "Treasures of a Worshipper". He shared with me that it was a collection of messages, quotes, and editorials preached or taught by his father, my brother Shawn. It sounded interesting, so I said, "send me your manuscript", thinking that it would be a sweet, perfunctory attempt of a young son trying to honor his father. When I received and started reading his manuscript, I was dumbfounded: BEYOND BELIEF!! His presentation, flow, and delivery were as if he had been writing for 20 years. Having written a couple of best sellers myself, I know firsthand the time and suffering it usually takes to mature and develop into a seasoned, accomplished writer.

My nephew writes with a fluidity, scope, and maturity well beyond his 25 years! Honestly, I had to repress feelings of envy towards "MY OWN NEPHEW", only because I wished I had possessed the sophistication of an author at his age. He has taken the thoughts of his father and masterfully constructed a manual that, if read and acted upon, will bless and expand the spiritual horizons of everyone who reads it.

My brother has always been a worshipper. His son certainly carries his "worship DNA"! They both realize the impetus behind God's desire to be praised and the necessity; but also privilege of every Child of God being used as an instrument to magnify the God of glory!

The lessons are palpable, the quotes are brilliant and thought provoking, and the content is God inspired. Anyone reading this "magnus opus" will be inspired to search out and reap the benefits that come with being a worshipper.

Finally, "qualis pater talis filius" is Latin for "Like father like son". If there ever was a template that suggested that C. Shawn Tyson & James Edison Tyson, II carry the same unique and profound anointing, it can be realized in *Treasures of a Worshipper*. Read, be inspired, and glean from two men who have personally experienced the divine blessings and benedictions found in being in the presence of an exalted Jesus!

-J. LaVerne Tyson

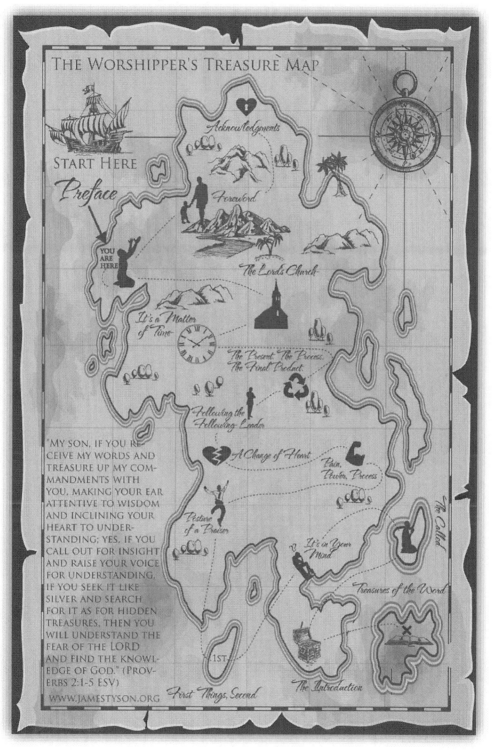

Preface

"PRESERVE YOUR FATHER'S VOICE..."

Saturday, December 31, 2011. Seated in what could have been one of the most impactful services of my entire life, I watched my father, Bishop C. Shawn Tyson, mount the sacred podium, as I have my entire life to declare the infallible word of the living God. The message: "When Walls Fall Down" (scriptural reference: Joshua 6:1-2,10).[1] I witnessed the audience that gathered for our New Year's Eve Celebration, or what many know as "Watch Night Service", erupt in sheer pandemonium as this man, being controlled by the Spirit of God, leaned back, right leg suspended in the air and right hand covering his right ear, released a yell (holler, if you will) that shook Calvary Ministries International. Seated in the back corner of the choir stand, tears began streaming down my face. The authority, power, and conviction by which my father ministered caused my eyes to be fixated upon him while simultaneously being constrained to my seat, not by any physical object; but I was constrained by the voice of the Lord planting the seed in my heart for what you are preparing to read.

---

[1] See "Treasurers in The Word" chapter to read the scripture text in its entirety.

Please bear in mind, the year 2011 could have easily been one of the most challenging years of my entire life. Just a few months prior to this service, July 6th to be exact, my grandfather, the Honorable Bishop James E. Tyson, transitioned from labor to reward. Anyone who has a relationship with me will tell you that my grandfather was and is one of the most influential men in my life. A hero. From birth to age nineteen, our relationship was more along the lines of a "father and son" rather than "grandfather and grandson". When referencing our relationship, my father would often tell others, "He's more his grandfather's son than mine." Transparently speaking, losing him created somewhat of a dark cloud over my head. That is not to say I was not happy my grandfather could rest and be with the Lord in peace; rather, his absence left a tremendous void in my heart that could not be filled with kind words, hugs, or any one individual. I was hurt. The kind of hurt that leaves you wandering the halls of a hotel during an international convention and finding a seat in a corner of the lobby that would become your personal mourning station. The type of hurt that leaves you shaking as you sit on the bathroom floor attempting to do everything in your power to refrain from having a nervous breakdown. No one could change it or reverse it; pain consumed me. Needless to say, at the conclusion of a difficult year, I wanted to leave the pain in 2011. I just did not want to leave my grandfather.

As the power of God is exploding in the sanctuary like an atomic bomb, I hear the voice of the Lord whisper in my ear as if He were seated in the seat next to me, "Preserve your father's voice in the Earth." My emotions began flaring. I could not manage another one "taken" from me. I felt as if God was using me as his punching bag. I was under the natural assumption that the Lord was getting ready to take my father, just as He did my grandfather; both of my heroes, gone? That was a load I was not prepared to carry. It was not until I began moving beyond my emotions, that I began receiving the instructions.

What you are preparing to read is the preservation of legacy. It is a collection of treasures from the Lord through a worshipper. In his book of wisdom, Solomon illustrates to the reader the significance and blessings of wisdom through a conversation between a father and son. The Bible shares with us this dialogue in Proverbs 2:1-5 KJV.[2] It says,

> "[1]My son, if thou wilt receive my words, and hide my commandments with thee; [2]So that thou incline thine ear unto wisdom, and apply thine heart to understanding; [3]Yea, if thou criest after knowledge, and liftest up thy voice for understanding; [4]If thou seekest her as silver, and searchest for her as for hid treasures; [5]Then shalt thou understand the fear of the Lord, and find the knowledge of God."

The father deposits in the mind of his son to equate knowledge and wisdom to that of silver and hidden treasures. It becomes essential for you, the reader, to comprehend that in your hands is much more than "just

---

[2] See "Treasurers in The Word" chapter to read the scripture text in its entirety.

another book". You hold one of the most valuable assets you will ever possess on Earth. Wisdom.

I recall vividly my father addressing an audience of notable religious leaders, dignitaries, and aspiring men and women who were seeking the same treasure in this compilation. Removing his glasses and glaring into the very soul of every man and woman in the room, he says, "The greatest title you will ever have is not Bishop, Pastor, Elder, CEO, President, or Leader. The greatest title and the only title you can take with you to heaven is 'worshipper'. When I die, if they call me nothing else, I want them to call me a worshipper." My friend, hidden within the pages of this book are over thirty years of wisdom concerning various topics for all, no matter what your current stage of life, occupation, vocation, or spiritual state. I caution you: What you are getting ready to be exposed to has the potential to change your life and the lives of anyone with whom you share these treasures, whether within your home, church, or on the job.

At the end of every chapter you will find a space called "Treasure Reflections". I encourage you to use this space and take the opportunity to capture what has been deposited into your mind, life, and spirit. Write and reflect upon what you have learned, areas in your life that need improvement, and what God spoke to you concerning that topic. Add these reflections to your treasure chest and build your life, one jewel at a time. It is my earnest prayer that these treasures will be a blessing to you, as they have been to me and many around the world. Prepare the digging trowels and shovels of your mind as we embark upon our search in the *Treasures of a Worshipper*.

Chapter 1

THE LORD'S CHURCH

Proceeding the revelation of Jesus as the Christ, Jesus tells Simon Bar-jona in Matthew 16:18 KJV[3], "*And I say also unto thee, That thou art Peter, and upon this rock I will build my church; and the gates of hell shall not prevail against it.*" So often in modern colloquialism, more specifically in religious circles, you hear the phrase, "The church is under attack." Often, when I hear this being said, the questions that come to my mind fall in an order such as this: "Who or what is attacking the church? What about 'the church' is 'it' attacking? Whose church are we referencing? Are we referencing the Lord's church or man's concept of 'the church'?" All of the aforementioned questions are critical and necessary to answer when considering the church being under attack. If, when addressing the attack of the church, we are referring to "The Lord's Church", then it should come as no surprise that the enemy is conceptualizing every plot he can formulate within his genius to overpower and conquer the Lord's church. Jesus shares with Peter, "the gates of hell shall not prevail against it"; however, the lack of prevailing by satanic forces will not hinder any of its attempted pursuits. There are strategies, methodologies, and ideas in the arsenal of Satan that are targeted directly at every component of the Lord's church. Racial division, the collapse of the nuclear family, an epidemic of title chasing, a lack of love, and degrading of

---

[3] See "Treasurers in The Word" chapter to read the scripture text in its entirety.

JAMES E. TYSON, II

holy living in an effort to be socially acceptable are all examples of the devices Satan uses to gain an advantage over the Lord's church. So, to reference the pursuit of destruction upon the Lord's church as if it is a new idea or creative effort on the part of Satan and his angels is entirely inaccurate. As long as the Lord's church stands, it will be the enemy of Satan.

So, what is "the Lord's church"? The first mention of the word "church" in the Bible is found in the previously referenced scripture (Matthew 16:18). There are several key factors that one must identify when considering the Lord's church. Firstly, the establishment of the Lord's church was initiated by the revelation of who Jesus is. Without the awareness of the identity of the establishmentarian, or Jesus as God and Christ, one lacks a full comprehension of the characteristics of the Lord's church. Whenever an inventor or author creates, he or she does not merely formulate a product or service. Rather, this inventor is releasing an extension of himself or herself. It is an idea, concept, or thought that has been meticulously manufactured into what the creator has imagined. Steve Jobs, an American information technology entrepreneur and inventor, was not merely masterful at formulating products, but revolutionizing and disrupting society's concept of technology. His passion created extensions of himself ranging from the Macintosh to the iPhone. The indelible imprint of Steve Jobs' identity was ingrained in every product he produced. The same thought is applicable to the Lord's church. Any characteristics of the church that are not in alignment with the characteristics of Jesus lack the true authenticity of its original design. If Jesus is love, holiness, righteousness, and peace, His church should strive toward the attributes of its founder.

Another foundational truth concerning the Lord's church is that it is THE LORD'S CHURCH. Jesus was very clear in His conversation with Peter, "...upon this rock I will build my church..." Too often the Lord's church becomes personality driven which ultimately shifts the praise from the creator of man to the created man. My spirit shudders at the sight of men and women strapping on their tool belts, attempting reconstruct the spiritual structure of the Lord's church. In no way do I condemn new methods that retain the central message of Jesus to win souls to Christ and develop an individual into a holistic Christian. However, when the words of Jesus become whited out and an individual signs their name with the ink of pride and ego on the title deed to the Lord's church, we have treaded on dangerous territory. To a degree, it is quite remarkable how not only will the leader place himself or herself above the Lord, but the followers (some unknowingly) can place their leader before the Lord. This highlights the necessity of having and emphasizing a God-centered and God-focused ministry.

Since the inception of the Lord's church, many have attempted to recreate an identity for her (by "her", I'm referencing the Lord's church) that is not congruent with its standards, morals, concepts, systems, environment, culture, or most importantly, Jesus. These treasures bring us into focus on the purpose, power, practices, and principles of the Lord's church.

Do not pollute the sound of Pentecost by division.

Christianity is not a religion of convenience, but it is a relationship on conviction.

We need to put our traditions aside, get together, get to God, and get back on one accord. THIS IS the will of God.

How is that the world can come together regardless of race, creed or color to PARTY, but the church can't do the same to come together to PRAY?

Until the church goes color blind, we will never see the full measure of the glory of God!

Memo to all "Sunday Morning Only Saints": Most of the answers you are searching for can be found at BIBLE CLASS.

Don't allow selfish people with their self-righteous attitude convince you to be a part of perpetuating division in the body of Christ.

Being a great church today does not mean you will be a great church tomorrow if you don't maintain your aggression in prayer, worship, soul-

*winning and effective ministry
development.*

*God is the one in the driver's seat in the
car of destiny.*

*Christ is not just a part of our lives, but
He is our lives.*

*The size of the church does not
determine the significance of their
assignment.*

*A good amen corner will shift the whole
house! Your vocal response to truth
releases the spirit of truth in the house.*

*Those who have no respect of persons
respect all people.*

*The most dangerous spirit in the
church is the spirit of Uzzah. That is the
spirit that presumes upon the presence
of God and imposes one's familiarity
with spiritual things.*

It's dangerous to be redundant in rituals because you can be in one place and God be in another without you. Don't let church ruin you.

If the church will go to the world, the world will come to the church.

When you don't come to church just because the pastor did not come to church that means that God's presence is not worth your presence.

If the young people refuse to stand up the whole church will fall down.

The Lord has us in a season where the church no longer needs to be sermonized, but revolutionized.

Sometimes the significance of simple truth is overlooked in the pursuit of more complex ideas in the advancement of the 21st century church.

It is up to the sons whether the church will become a monument or a movement.

The church assists you in growing in the faith both through the fellowship of the saints and through the covering of a pastor.

Churches that are bigger are not always better.

It is not long after saints get mixed in with sinners that they become mixed up in foolishness.

We give an unbalanced perspective on the mercy of God. We talk about the heavenly places, but not the hellish places that God prepares for saints.

Saints don't chase blessings. Blessings chase saints.

Being at maximum performance does not mean you should be in church 7 days a week, but it does mean you should walk in the spirit 24 hours a day.

The church cannot condone what God condemns.

Changing the laws ain't gonna change God's mind.

Your doctrine is null and void if you're not living according to the Law of Love.

Having the right "doctrine' won't help you if your HEART is still wrong!

Church is great, but change is greater.

If you can't serve the people of God, you can't lead the people of God.

God calls you to discover the greatness in others to make them greater than you.

Action always begins with compassion.

Great men pray while good men sleep.

If you're not willing to be challenged then you're not ready to be changed.

For God so loved the world THAT HE GAVE! Living in this world is not enough. The question is, what are you GIVING to the world? It is impossible to be a REAL CHRISTIAN and be selfish. You're not living if you're not giving.

Some of us have been in church so long we forgot who God is.

Let the glory of the Lord be so bright in you that if the sun never shined again, the world would still have light.

*You cannot have kingdom principles
without kingdom pursuit.*

*There is no manipulation in love, only
transparency.*

*You cannot do a spiritual thing a
natural way.*

*Clean (religious) spirits can be more
lethal to the operation of spiritual
things than unclean spirits.*

*Real Christians always care more
about the solutions to other people's
problems than answers to their own
questions.*

You must think eternally.

*Whenever an environment is created to
please people, outward appearance
becomes more important than inward
reality.*

*Do not assume that just because you
are in a church setting that everybody
came looking for Jesus.*

Treasure Reflections

_____

_____

_____

_____

_____

_____

_____

_____

_____

_____

_____

_____

_____

_____

_____

_____

_____

_____

_____

_____

_____

_____

Chapter 2

IT'S A MATTER OF TIME

"We are now faced with the fact that tomorrow is today. We are confronted with the fierce urgency of now. In this unfolding conundrum of life and history, there *is* such a thing as being too late. This is no time for apathy or complacency. This is a time for vigorous and positive action." In these impactful words, Dr. Martin L. King, Jr. captures, as does the word of God (read Ecclesiastes 3:1-8),[4] one of the most valuable commodities we will ever have: time. Time, provided by the creator of time, affords us the opportunity to fulfill our goals, aspirations, and purpose. I am a firm believer that, along with destiny, each of us have been given the gift of time; however, the danger of said gift is its misuse or lack of use by the receiver. Very quickly, a gift with such value as time, one that is designed to aid you in life, will aid you in regret if not appropriately applied. It is incumbent upon us that we learn our own identity and then effectively manage and master time within it. The late, great Dr. Myles Munroe once said, "Where purpose is not known, abuse in inevitable." Management of time must begin with the searching, understanding, and operation of one's purpose; otherwise,

---

[4] See "Treasurers in The Word" chapter to read the scripture text in its entirety.

you will be in an abusive relationship with your life, time, gifts, and abilities for the remainder of your life. I share with as many as I can while traveling this country, that one of the greatest tragedies a person could experience would be to live an entire lifetime and not know themselves one day. Often, we live as successful representatives of ourselves; not really living, but just acting and wasting time while we are merely casting in this stage play called "Life".

An essential key to mastering time is located in this hidden truth (please repeat these words after me): "I don't know how much time I have." A hard reality? Yes. Manageable? Absolutely. Unless you have such a relationship with Jesus that, within you, He has placed a spiritual clock that, when you awake every morning, it shows you the number of years, months, weeks, days, hours, minutes, and seconds you have remaining in life or before His imminent return, you do not know how much time you have. Properly grasping and understanding this concept has enough force behind it to motivate you to live today like there is no tomorrow. George Bernard Shaw, Irish playwright and socialist, said, "Youth is wasted on the young." While I agree with the concept and perception Shaw gives on time, it becomes the choice of the reader to either accept it as their personal truth or defy the status quo. Being able to view youth within the parameters of "vitality and ability", rather than "extra time and substantial opportunity", will create a distinction between those who wisely use time and those who abuse time.

While using "time" is of utmost importance, of equal importance is having an understanding of "the time". Before I continue, let's expound on my use of the word "understanding". In this sense, to understand means to perceive, recognize, or discern. Without proper understanding (perception, recognition, or discernment) one's concept of time and the times will be misconstrued. You see, there is a distinct difference between the two. Knowing what time it is focuses primarily upon chronological time; however, "the time" focuses on seasons, experiences, and occasions. In short, "time" changes, but "the time" shifts. I remember my father teaching me as a young boy, that there is a significant difference between knowing the right thing to do and knowing the right time to do it. Let's pause here and make a decree together. Repeat these words: "I will have the advantage! This year, I will not be behind, miss cues, or postpone deadlines. I will be, live, function, and operate on schedule!"

Having understanding of the time is not only critical for your movement, but also the movement of those in your immediate sphere of influence. I must reiterate a vital principle; underline, highlight, circle, or take a picture of it. Please get this in your mind and spirit because, once you do, it will change your perspective on life. "The advantage is always on the side of those who have the understanding of the times and those who know the best course of action to take." It is not enough to hear the time, know the time, and yield to the time; but, you must have understanding of the time to know how to govern your actions, decisions, career pursuits, spirit walk, and even your goal planning.

Let's continue searching for the treasure of wisdom found in the words of a worshipper concerning time, timing, and the times. Are you ready? Let's dig!

Failure to act in the time of activation will result in promises pending.

A level of a man's revelation of spiritual things is not based upon why he hears in the present moment, but based upon the application of what he has already heard in the past.

Lot's wife's first look backward was her last step forward. Be careful about trying to go back to what God brought you out of.

You cannot live life in rewind.

What you are willing to let go will determine what God is willing to let come. It's old school technology.

Today God is saying if you want to get where I'm trying to take you, get your finger off that rewind button and push fast-forward!

I don't know who came up with the saying "here today gone tomorrow". I told the church we're not going ANYWHERE until God says so. Don't let the enemy punk you. The devil doesn't make our calendar. I shall not be moved! Here today...Here Tomorrow.

Don't die one second before your time.

3 words to walk in today: Activation. Manifestation. Momentum.

Sometimes God does things twice to show that He's still the God of "again".

Whatever you need God to do again, He already did it.

It's time to stop crying over your past and start rejoicing over your future.

GOD can do in ONE DAY what you've been trying to do without Him the entire year. Step back! Let God do it!

If you're not thinking about the future, the only thing left to define you is the past.

It's possible for a positive person to have a negative moment.

Just be patient. You're about to arrive to a place called promise.

God is not living in the moment, but always living in and trying to bring us into the next moment.

Nothing has come to pass that God has not already thought or allowed.

Never allow the interval between the beginning and the end make you lose confidence in God's promises toward you.

There cannot be manifestation until there is instruction.

There is nothing worse than a person with no timing. Timing is not innate, but timing is learned.

The reason why access has been delayed is because it was ready for you, but you weren't ready for it.

God knows the cause and the effect of everything that happens in our lives and He orchestrates them to bring Him glory.

It's already prepared for you; you've got to get prepared for it.

You have to be ready because time won't wait.

Suddenly, now means immediately, which means right now!

The instability of your past will not prevent the stability of your present and future.

Refocus your mind to the goals and the timelines to which you must complete them.

It is possible to redeem time, but not a moment in time.

We can seize and master the moment, or deny the moment.

Every moment in time must be defined.

Time is life's most valuable commodity because you never know when you are going to run out of it.

The Lord says, stop using prayer as your excuse for procrastination. You don't need to pray on it, you've already done that. You need to ACT ON IT!

When you don't use time wisely you are wasting life foolishly.

Access today does not guarantee access tomorrow.

We are in the present, what we thought in the past.

When God has a plan that originated in eternity that will reveal itself in time, and on a time schedule, your prayers will not preempt the plan of God.

Joy and sorrow cannot occupy the same soul at the same time.

Time management will be more essential this year than any other time to date.

We must take quality time with our best friend to find out what's on His mind.

Understanding of the times must be the beginning of the fulfillment of purpose.

If you cannot locate God where you are, if the lines of communication are temporarily disconnected, sometimes you have to retrace your steps back to the last time God had a hold to your spirit, mind, and body.

There is a time to speak and a time to be quiet, but never a time to be negative.

Time does not determine identity. Purpose determines identity.

People that are concentrating on their future, don't have time to think about their past.

It's time for you to step up!

Do not assume this is just another time, when it could be the last time!

You're not always going to know why, where or what you're going to, but purpose will not be revealed until you get to the destined place that God has chosen to reveal it.

Whatever you do, don't allow your frustration to kill the promise in the process. I know the last instruction looked like destruction, but keep listening, God has another instruction.

<u>Treasure Reflections</u>

_____

_____

_____

_____

_____

_____

_____

_____

_____

_____

_____

_____

_____

_____

_____

_____

_____

_____

_____

_____

_____

_____

_____

_____

Chapter 3

THE PRESENT. THE PROCESS. THE FINAL
PRODUCT.

Throughout my life, I have always been a "results-driven" person. Whenever I was working on a project, attempting to achieve a spiritual goal, and even providing for my wife and son; in my mind, if I did not see some type of immediate results, I did not think it was working. I suppose you can liken my thinking (I speak in present-tense because it is a day-to-day recalibration of the mind) to an impatient planter planting a seed. He/she takes the effort to dig in the soil, appropriately place the seed into the ground, cover it again with the soil, and water it. Then after five minutes of impatiently waiting, he/she slips into an overwhelming state frustration that exudes through their obnoxious whining, beating the ground profusely, and shaking their fist at the sky as if the sun was to slow to provide heat and the clouds weren't cooperating to provide rain. Seems somewhat oxymoronic, doesn't it?

Interestingly, many are like this impatient planter, both in a natural and spiritual context. Often, we can become so preoccupied with attempting to obtain physical evidence of the end result, that we miss the tremendous blessing of patiently enduring the process. Jesus said, *"In your patience possess ye your souls"* (Luke 21:19 KJV).[5] Patiently enduring the process will yield appreciation for the final product. So easy is it to become discouraged as you are making strides toward destiny, educational pursuits, and career endeavors, especially when life happens. Everyone reading this book will not be able to comprehend my last statement depending upon their stage in life; however, for others who have endured the George Foreman-like blow that life sends crashing upon your mind and spirit, seeing the sunshine behind dark clouds can be a challenge. Though some will refuse to admit it, many become spiritually depleted daily because the spiritual fight they are engaged in, ultimately, can make heaven feel out of reach. When life comes knocking on your bedroom door and all kinds of negative thoughts climb into bed with you, attempting to rock you into a state of depression and doubt, believing that there is light in this darkness seems more difficult as the moments go by. It would appear that you're alone and no one quite understands the incomprehensible pain you have to deal with just to open your eyes. Do me a favor and answer this question in the margin: Have you ever reached a stage in life where prayers just became tears and short sentences such as, "Jesus, help me!" "God, where are you?" "I need you!" Yeah, me too. While our experiences may be different, the principles of our process remain the same in our natural and spiritual lives. You see, you're better off with Jesus on your worst day than you are anywhere else on your best

---

[5] See "Treasurers in The Word" chapter to read the scripture text in its entirety.

day. The beauty of the process is that God out of sight is not God out of presence. Psalm 46:1 says, *"God is our refuge and strength, a very present help in trouble."*[6] Let me share this story with you.

Prior to my wife and I getting married, she lived in Forestville, MD, which is right outside of Washington, DC. For me, living in Youngstown, OH, at the time, I would have to drive somewhere between 4.5 to 5.5 hours depending upon construction and good 'ol D.C./Maryland traffic (which I hate with all my heart, soul, and mind). I never quite knew where I was going, but thank and praise God for the navigation system. I relied on it heavily as I traveled to the city and also while in the city. Generally, if I travel somewhere frequently, I try to create markers for myself so I know how much further I have to go. In route to Washington, D.C., you have to drive on the PA Turnpike for close to 85-90 miles. On the turnpike, in route to my half-way marker (Breezewood, PA), there is a tunnel that stretches about a mile and a half. You know, one of those tunnels that are only two lanes and you have to stay in your designated lane. Each time I would go through the tunnel, my navigation system would lose signal. The first few times while traveling to Maryland, I panicked because I was in a tunnel that looked like Jason and Freddy Krueger could walk out at any moment. I had never been this way before, and I was dependent upon my navigation system to talk me through these mountains. After traveling this way several times, I discovered that if I just keep driving through this

---

[6] See "Treasurers in The Word" chapter to read the scripture text in its entirety.

Twilight Zone looking tunnel, when I get to the end of it, my navigation system would locate a signal and continue giving me directions. I also found, after the navigation system received a signal, that even through the tunnel, I was still going in the right direction. I just had to get through it to get where I needed to go.

The same principle applies to appreciating your process. In life, you can easily become frustrated like me, traveling down a road you have never been, and going through tunnels just trying to reach destiny. On the way, it seems like your navigation system loses its signal in your home, career, and spiritual life. However, if you can just get through the tunnel, you'll soon find that while your environment looks odd, you are traveling in the right direction. The key is not to pull over just because your surroundings make a drastic shift. Please, don't stop in the middle of the process! You will make it to the other side, but your focus must remain on the end product of what you will become and not on where you are presently.

As you begin searching for treasures, allow each jewel to encourage you in your process, both in your natural and spiritual life. Get your tools; you're going to need what you find. Teddy Roosevlt once said, "Champions don't become champions in the ring, they are merely recognized there."

***You must have confidence in order to
get to the next step in destiny.***

***My moment will not determine my
eternity.***

Be ye also ready! When the rapture happens, there will be no re-runs.

I'm not worried about being a "star". I just want to be a light.

You cannot embrace the future, clinging to the past.

Lot's wife represents the individual that insists on looking back when God has more life in front of you.

Your best life is still in front of you!

Looking back at something God gave you can prove to be fatal when God takes it away from you.

It's already done!

No man can put a period in your life where God has put a comma.

Sin is not the only thing that can prevent you from fulfilling your purpose.

Nothing less than our best will be acceptable unto God in this season of the supernatural.

Eternity is too long to be wrong!

We will not be able to walk in the kingdom authority like our fathers until we walk in the kingdom righteousness as our fathers.

I am being prepared during a season of persecution for unparalleled progress.

Fear not! God has already made provisions for you to prosper in life, love, and in your pursuit of happiness.

I see me debt free!

*Despite what you see, God's promises
will still come to pass the way He said
it.*

*The sooner you realize you can't fix it,
the sooner God will.*

*Determined in eternity. Purposes are made manifest in
time.*

Don't abort God's process in your life.

*Most people don't know what they can
do because they've only been told what
they could not do.*

*God's about to move you from
contentment to fulfillment.*

*God will give us the resources we need
to start and finish, but the first
resource we need is faith.*

Why God brought you into this world determines your conduct, your movement, and your mission.

Anticipate revelation beyond expectations.

Seeing is the beginning of being. All manifestations require maturation.

Greatness is your only option!

Never be so focused on where you have to go next that you miss where God has you now.

This must be the year that you come all the way back into the secret place of God. The first place you must begin that pursuit is in your worship.

In this season, you must make the decision to live in fear or in faith, but you cannot live in both.

The universe and our continued existence are dependent upon God and His control.

Visions should always be written down. That way, you will be able to gauge the process of the vision.

The difference between an idea and a vision is a pen. Until the vision is written down, it has not met the biblical criteria of being a vision.

In faith, there is no past and no future, there is only present. "[7]Now faith is the substance of things hoped for, the evidence of things not seen."

You're getting close to the finish line.

---

[7] See "Treasurers in The Word" chapter to read the scripture text in its entirety.

Your past can only define you if you choose to live in it.

You don't even know how you got in it, but God is going to bring you out of it.

Embrace the responsibility of legacy.

You are already on God's schedule for an impending comeback.

Don't allow what has happened to change your expectation of what God said.

Your value to the kingdom of light determines your value to the kingdom of darkness.

What you did is not who you are.

Do not forsake doing the right thing in order to pursue a course of action that will compromise or jeopardize your

destiny because you are frustrated where you are.

Just be patient. You're about to arrive to a place called promise.

It is what breaks you that makes you.

God is depending on you to be great!

The absence of a plan at the beginning of any endeavor guarantees failure at the end.

Have a proper perspective of God's view for your life.

Celebrate legacy by fulfilling your destiny.

Whether you live or die, prosper or perish, this year will be determined by what you say about tomorrow, today.

Treasure Reflections

Chapter 4

FOLLOW THE FOLLOWING-LEADER

Former President, the late John F. Kennedy, said, "Leadership and learning are indispensable to each other." Without the capacity to learn, you have disqualified yourself to lead. Leadership, as a topic and as it pertains to individuals, is something that I am extremely passionate about and over the 20th and 21st centuries, both in the religious and secular circles, it has made dramatic shifts; some for the betterment of leadership and others to its detriment. In the early 1900's, leadership primarily emphasized control and the centralization of power. It had absolutely nothing to do with inspiration or the development of followers, but rather, everything to do with domination. Sadly, some are still fixated on that ineffective style of leadership. As time progressed, the face of leadership began shifting from control to influence (i.e. being driven by who an individual is), and defining good leadership by how well a leader's group is developing. Then, it began making a turn toward being defined as "excellent" according to the traits of that leader (i.e. height, gender, race, age, etc.).

Finally, this roller coaster turns us to this major technological age in which we live during this 21st century. As leadership has evolved, its definition has also evolved. Thus far, researchers have been able to agree upon this understanding: Leadership is a process whereby an individual influences a group of individuals to achieve a common goal (Northouse 2001). Scholars tend to suggest that there are six major traits that leaders should possess including: intelligence, self-confidence, determination, integrity, sociability, and emotional intelligence. While I agree that the aforementioned qualities should be a part of an effective leader, there is one unmentioned quality that stands above them all and that is obedience.

In my humble estimation, the quality of obedience and the ability to humbly obey are the differentiating factors between a good leader and a great leader. In fact, the sign of an effective servant (because the responsibility of leadership is to serve) is the ability to master being obedient. Why would obedience be of such preeminence to the Lord? Well, consider the first man, Adam. What caused Adam and Eve to fall was not walking toward the tree of the knowledge of good and evil or even conversation with the serpent; nor was it touching the fruit. While all of these things led to the ultimate death or separation between God and man, the instruction was *"...thou shalt not eat of it..."* (See Genesis 2:17). [8] It was man's disobedience that initiated death or separation between God and man. So, we can now see why obedience is so dear to the heart of God. Please catch the principle: The root of effective leadership is not how well can you give an instruction, but rather how well you can follow an instruction. In short, this concept is called "selfless obedience."

---

[8] See "Treasurers in The Word" chapter to read the scripture text in its entirety.

When you consider a leader, what characteristics would you say he/she should possess? There is space provided below for you to jot down your thoughts.

_____

_____

_____

_____

_____

_____

In our consideration of leadership, characteristics such as intelligent, having integrity, or even being driven come to mind. If you were approaching leadership from a skills perspective, you might consider technical, human, or conceptual skills; however, I want you to consider the difference between how we choose leadership and how God chooses leadership. One of the most significant lessons you will learn as it pertains to the Lord and leadership (of which I am a product myself) is that when God chooses a leader, He never chooses the obvious. He always chooses the obedient. You remember tall, dark, and handsome Eliab, the brother of the psalmist, David? When the prophet Samuel saw him, he had a presumptuous thought that royalty was standing before him because of Eliab's exterior. Based upon the requirements of the nation and its previous leader, Eliab seemed like the obvious choice; however, there was a king with the sheep that was not in the company of the other sons who would be God's choice. What a misconception this story reveals to us! The presumptive perspective of Samuel has become a strange epidemic amongst those who should be spiritual people.

God does not operate from a mold or a preconstructed blueprint of the exterior characteristics of a leader. His diversification is too magnanimous to be relegated to a box. Take a look around you. Every tree, living creature, body of water, even the individual grains of sand were all constructed in the mind of God uniquely. His leaders are no exception. Too often we miss the Davids, focusing on the Eliabs, Abinadabs, and Shammahs. Wow, consider this thought with me. A Bible without David? Psalms without David? Generations without David? No David, no Jesus.[9] Spiritual rule of thumb: If they are the least likely to man, they're the most likely to God.

In fact, the scriptures specify that he was the "youngest." To see that word, "youngest" and merely apply it to the chronological age of David in comparison to his brothers is correct, but not complete. Take another look with me. In Hebrew, "youngest" is defined as "young, small, insignificant, or unimportant." Can I share with you something that changed my life? Never allow someone else's perspective to block your purpose. You were never gifted, anointed, or called according to perspective. Truthfully, if that was our reality, I, along with many others, would be disqualified from doing anything for the Lord. There are two thoughts that matter: what God thinks about you and what you think about you. God always has positive

---

[9] See "Treasurers in The Word" chapter to read the scripture text in its entirety.

thoughts about you (read Jeremiah 29:11) [10] no matter what stage of life you have been in or are in presently; however, the fulfillment of God's positive thoughts about you can be hindered or suppressed by your negative thoughts about yourself. At some point in your life, you have to stop being your own worst enemy and become a friend to your destiny. Take a moment and answer these questions. Before you write one word or even consider one sphere of thought, please leave dishonesty at the following period. Change of mind cannot be actualized with altered truths or fabricated realities. Own your truth.

How does God see you?

_____

_____

_____

_____

_____

_____

How do you see yourself?

_____

_____

_____

_____

---

[10] See "Treasurers in The Word" chapter to read the scripture text in its entirety.

Here's how many of us disqualify ourselves from doing great exploits in life and in the Lord: Many times, we allow what we consider to be "humility" to really be a hindrance to confidence. Don't miss the concept of what I am sharing with you. So often I hear, especially in religious circles, "We're not worthy" or "Who I am that God would use me to lead anything?" My responses to those statements are: "We're not" and "You're the chosen." This is where our concept of humility conflicts with possibility. Many tend to maximize on their frailty, humanity, or underdeveloped gifts. We deflect them on God, causing us to be self-destructive. Being meek does not mean you have to be weak and being humble does not mean you lose all confidence. In short, stop throwing yourself under the bus and allow your perspective to shift to God's thoughts toward you. If He chose you to lead them or this, then He trusts you to follow Him. Remember the principle: God does not choose the obvious, He chooses the obedient. If you are going to be effective and impactful as a leader, there are treasures that you will need along the way that are going to be beneficial to you. You know what I have discovered in life and leadership? Learning lessons does not have to consist of me repeatedly banging my head against a brick wall. If I carefully examine the knots on someone else's head and how they acquired golf ball sized bumps, then I can use their experience to my benefit. Do you have your equipment ready? What treasures does God reveal to us from a worshipper concerning leadership? Looks like we have more digging to do. Go for gold!

Leadership is not about getting people to do what YOU want them to do. It is about preparing and releasing them to do what GOD has created them to do. Don't ever confuse being people's leader with being their Lord.

Someone said, "If there is no one following you, you're not a leader." I say, "If there is no one LEADING you, you're not a qualified leader" because it doesn't matter how many people are following you; leaders still need LEADERSHIP AND COVERING.

Listening to people who are not listening to God is EXTREMELY dangerous, because folk will talk you INTO some "MESS" that they can't talk you out of and then disappear.

Until you learn how to be LED by the Holy Spirit, all the tongue talking in the world won't keep you out of sin. Talking in the Spirit (speaking in tongues) is important, but LISTENING to the Spirit and obeying His

instruction is what makes you a son of God.

Anybody can have a moment but don't let your moment turn into a day, a week, a month or into a year.

Leaders have to be able to function at a higher level of immediacy and efficiency.

You will never be a great public evangelist until you first become a great personal evangelist.

When great leaders die, great ministries should continue to live.

Identity must be found in God, not the leader. The leader determines direction, but God determines identity.

When you have a big vision, you must be surrounded by people with big minds.

*Greatness will always cost you
something.*

*Always keep God as the face and focal
point of the ministry.*

*Unless you give God's people something
to look forward to, they will always
have something to look backward to.*

*"Was great" does not translate into "is
great" or "will be great."*

*You cannot be great surrounded by
average people.*

*Leaders are born to be made leaders
before they were ever born.*

You are not too young to lead.

How you are prepared for leadership will determine where you stand. You cannot sit down with dummies and stand up with doctors.

10 Characteristics of the 21st century Leader: Prayerful, Character, Dedication, Flexibility, Teachability, Humility, Patience, Poise under pressure, Creativity, and Magnanimity.

Vision does not happen incidentally.

It's time for you to step up. People cannot be served until you show up for work.

Vision is the art of seeing invisible things.

When you are called to leadership, although you may be with everyone else, you will know early on that you are not like everyone else.

You cannot sit in a position of power if you do not have the power.

The call to lead does not eliminate the necessity to follow.

The power of the Holy Ghost is needed more on Monday than it is on Sunday. On Sunday, we are worshippers, but on Monday we must become witnesses. Unless our worship on Sunday inspires us to be a witness on Monday, our religion is in vain.

Obeying God isn't always the easy thing to do, but it's always the right thing to do.

If you are going to be on God's agenda then you must first eliminate all excuses. Find a reason to get it done!

No real Christian can condone what the Bible condemns.

Never become so content with where you are that you forget who you are and conform to an environment where it becomes impossible to be obedient to God's word. Remind yourself who you are!

You protect your kingdom by not disobeying the law of God.

Doing the will of God will always cost you something, but it's a lot less expensive than the price of disobedience.

You can't have perfect peace without perfect obedience.

When the pursuit of things takes precedent over the pursuit of God, you have unwillingly taken yourself out of alignment with the will of God, demoting you to "some things" instead of "all things."

A sprinkle of doubt, in God's word, is sin.

I will not repeat, but I will repent!

The question is not, "does God love you enough to forgive your sin?" The question is, "do you love HIM enough to give up your sin?"

Knowing when to do is just as important as knowing what to do.

It's ok to seek new knowledge from the omniscient God, but if you're not obeying what He has said before, why should He reveal new revelation?

Just because you've been doing something the same way doesn't mean it's always been God's way.

The Holy Ghost does not make you do right; it gives you the power to do right.

When God makes a decision, He doesn't want my opinion, He wants my obedience!

In all things, God must have preeminence.

God does not give commands for the sake of compromise; only for the expectation of obedience, and disobedience is the deal breaker.

If you never pay attention to the details in your life you will never fulfill the destiny for your life. Destiny is fulfilled not by leaps and bounds, but by one act of obedience at a time.

God does not need an addendum to His commandment or my opinion added to His decision. He needs our obedience.

Leadership is determined not by position, but by influence.

God's non-negotiable requirement for every servant leader is worship. Worship must be a personal priority and a persistent practice in your life in order to maximize the power, presence, and plan of God in your life and in the lives of those you are called to lead.

Treasure Reflections

_____

_____

_____

_____

_____

_____

_____

_____

_____

_____

_____

_____

_____

_____

_____

_____

_____

_____

_____

_____

_____

_____

Chapter 5

A CHANGE OF HEART

The heart is one of the two most important organs you have in your entire body. It is one of the main muscles, besides your brain, that is keeping your body alive. Elementary knowledge I would presume, right? In short, life or death is dependent upon the functionality of your heart. Allow me to repeat my last statement so it can settle in your mind. Life or death is dependent upon the functionality of your heart. This same concept of the heart is applicable in a spiritual context, as well as everyday life. The functionality and condition of your heart will determine your motives, effectiveness, and even the impact of your operation in spiritual things. The heart is an amazing thing. The scripture shares, *"Keep thy heart with all diligence; for out of it are the issues of life"* (Proverbs 4:23 KJV).[11] Another translation says, *"Guard your heart above all else, for it determines the course of your life"* (New Living Translation). How you manage or govern your life is a reflection of how you manage or govern your heart. What you have willingly or, unbeknownst to yourself, allowed in the inner recesses of your heart will be the determining factor of the direction of your life. "James, that seems to be

---

[11] See "Treasurers in The Word" chapter to read the scripture text in its entirety.

an over exaggeration. Don't you think?" No, I do not. Jeremiah wrote, *"The heart is deceitful above all things, and desperately wicked: who can know it?"* (Jeremiah 17:9 KJV).[12] Deceitful, in its context, means the heart is crooked and polluted. Yes, your heart has the potential to be crooked and polluted; causing the dysfunction of your life to be a direct product of heart disease. I know this is a book and it may seem a bit unorthodox to do so, but wherever you are whisper this prayer to the Lord, "Lord, help my heart."

So often we have heard it said or we have said ourselves, "Serve the Lord with all your heart, mind, and soul." While that is correct, I do not believe it is complete. You see, I can serve with all of my heart, but if my heart is selfish, it's of no effect. I can usher on the usher board with all my heart, but if I do not like people, my heart is going to show at the door. Your impact can go beyond the four walls of the church and spread into the boardroom, sports/entertainment, or medical profession, but if in your heart there is a lack of productivity and it is diseased with procrastination, nothing you do will be sustained. In Kingdom operation, your skill set may make you competent, but your heart will render you incompatible. Prior to entering full-time ministry, I had the opportunity to work in a variety of different industries including fast-food, banking, and transportation, just to name a few. On one of the jobs I worked during college, I had a coworker (in management might I add) who had the proper skills to

---

[12] See "Treasurers in The Word" chapter to read the scripture text in its entirety.

get a job done, but her heart was not in the work she produced. As a result, it made our establishment look poorly operated because she had an "I don't really care" attitude. It is incumbent upon us to ensure we properly examine our hearts, for out of it our ultimate end is determined.

Essentially, what it is going to take for your entire life to change is for you to have a change of heart. You could almost call it a heart transplant. I cannot stress enough that the critical component of this chapter is embedded in understanding that life or death is dependent upon the functionality of your heart. While you may have tried to avoid it, you have to now find out, "What is in my heart?" What have you permitted to take preeminence in your heart? Is it people? Mistakes? Your past?

Below I've provided a space for you to write an eviction notice to anything or anyone that may be preventing you from living and living in Christ.

EVICTION NOTICE (EFFECTIVE IMMEDIATELY):

_____

_____

_____

_____

_____

_____

The moment you are able to discover who or what has taken residence in the living room of your heart, the more you will be able to understand why you are at this stage of life. Remarkably, what you will find is that this is going to be one of the most difficult chapters for you to navigate. I know it was for me. When you really get to the root of why you are the way you are, why you do what you do, think how you think, and limit yourself the way you do; you will find that extracting it can be quite difficult. Why? Because roots have the potential to run deep.

I remember just a few years ago, I was teaching a series during youth Bible study to a group I had the opportunity to lead known as Dominion, the young people of Calvary Ministries International. The series was entitled, "I Got Over It". It was four weeks of intense teaching and tackling the hard subjects that have left tremendous wounds in our lives. Food for thought: I want to challenge all youth leaders/directors/pastors that if you haven't already, talk with and teach the youth of your assembly (with the permission of the Pastor) the taboo topics that many are not willing to discuss in a church setting. It is impossible to set "standards" when you are not willing to discuss "setbacks." I already know this is easier said than done for some; however, might I share with you a quote that I learned in a seminar that I now apply to any pursuit I attempt to accomplish? "The last seven words of every dying church, organization, or business are: 'We've never done it that way before.'" Well, I took my own advice and it navigated me to a completely unexpected, unanticipated, and truthfully, unwanted place.

During the final night of that series, the presence of the Lord filled that classroom in an indescribable way. I looked around the room and saw these young people with tears in their eyes, embracing one another, worshipping the Lord as their hearts, emotions, and spirits were being healed. The burden and heaviness that I had seen for several years had been lifted. Then, something unexpected happened. As I stood there, watching what I prayed for actually happen, it stirred up a wave of emotions and uncovered wounds in me that I did not realize still existed. In an effort to conceal it from the sight of the young people, I rushed to a dark classroom across the hall and sat in a corner. While sitting in that corner sobbing, hoping no one would hear me, the teacher became the student. For weeks, I taught Dominion how to heal and overcome pain from the past, but for years I trained myself how to suppress it, shoving it into a dark corner in my heart, never to be addressed again. This time, I was unsuccessful. Sometimes it is necessary for you to lose in order for you to win. Well, I lost. I lost the battle of hiding my infected wounds so that I could win, living a liberated life. One of the reasons we become so frustrated when certain things transpire in our lives, is not because of what someone else has done; but rather, it is because we waited so long to address this mountain of emotions and spiritual instability when it was a molehill.

Before you go further, take a moment and consider the matters of your heart. What is your "mountain"? As you discover these treasures, bear in mind that each one is one step further up the mountain that you will soon conquer. *"Keep thy heart with all diligence; for out of it are the issues of life" (Proverbs 4:23 KJV).*

Yes, God does love you, but that fact won't help you until YOU decide to love you.

Matters of the heart are always the heart of the matter when it comes to Jesus.

Do not serve Jesus with your head, but serve Him with your heart.

If you own anything that you cannot give away with gladness, you don't own it, it owns you.

Fulfillment without frustration comes by having kingdom centered motives.

Coming to church does not make God first in your heart. Becoming the church makes God first in your heart.

God's love is too valuable to be treated indifferently.

If you are doing all the giving, and they are doing all the taking, you are unequally yoked.

There are plenty of things out here for you to play with, but GOD ain't one of 'em!

It's what GOD said "NO" to that saved your life!

Never trust a person who does not trust God.

You don't lose true friends. If they left, that was just God letting your fake friend leave so your real friend could come.

You may have made a great mistake, but your great mistake is not greater than God's great grace.

If "EVERYBODY" likes you, you can cross GOD off that list.

Please don't walk out on your life and demand a refund. What you are going

through now is not the end, it's only the intermission. The rest of your life will be the best of your life!

I'm not living the rest of my life in misery!

If you have to wonder whether or not they are your friend...they're not!

Because God can do exceeding abundantly above all we can ask or think, God cannot tolerate being doubted.

Every time you run from a problem, you're also running from a solution.

Just because Jesus doesn't tell you what you want to hear doesn't mean He's not going to provide all of your needs.

You attract yourself to yourself. In other words, if you love you, you will

attract love to you. But if you hate yourself...love you first.

Never allow your fear to lie to your faith.

There is no such thing as an impotent thought.

Whatever you think yourself into, you can think yourself out of.

You can never be more or less than what you think about yourself.

You are the residual outcome of what you thought about yourself in the past.

What you attract is determined by the content and the quality of what you think.

You become a danger to yourself and a menace to society when you lose all consciousness of God.

The hardest decision you will ever make is to make the decision to move forward with God or remain stuck in the past with someone you love.

You have not yet seen the best you!

You cannot win if you expect to lose.

Don't use a public forum to try and settle a private issue. Never put your personal business in the street like that.

If you're not willing to be challenged then you're not ready to be changed.

When you truly love yourself, it becomes impossible to hate anyone else.

I don't care how many times they break your heart; don't let anyone break your spirit!

God has not forgotten about you. He both sees you and hears you.

Doing it God's way the FIRST TIME will save you a whole lot of unnecessary drama and pain. You won't have to learn "the hard way" if you learn God's way.

People resort to drama when they don't know their true identity.

If you are living in the past, you are dying in the present.

God doesn't always give you what you ask for, but He always gives you what you need.

Be careful about anyone who comes into a relationship making a whole lot of demands.

If I keep trying to do things my way, when will God have a chance to do things His way?

If you weren't so valuable, the devil wouldn't be trying so hard to take you out!

Until you have loved an enemy, you don't really know how to love a friend.

The one who left you is the one who really blessed you because greater can't come until lesser leaves.

Ask God to give you a change of heart.

If you don't know the inner workings of your heart, how are you going to determine the inward parts of another man's heart?

*You cannot criticize someone with
clean hands and you have a dirty heart.*

*If your doctrine is right and your heart
is wrong you will still lift up your eyes
in the lake of fire.*

*God will supply all your needs as soon
as you trust Him with all your heart.*

Treasure Reflections

_____

_____

_____

_____

_____

_____

_____

_____

_____

_____

_____

_____

_____

_____

_____

_____

_____

_____

_____

_____

_____

_____

_____

_____

_____

_____

_____

_____

Chapter 6

PAIN, POWER, PURPOSE

I believe that the Lord has blessed me with the greatest, first-born son in the world: my main man, Caden Shawn Tyson (who I affectionately call "Chief"). Outside of the occasions when the forces of the underworld crawl into his throat and he belts out a scream for dear life or when something deadly and viciously odorous captures the innocence of his diaper, he's amazing. I remember my wife, Desiree, and I taking Caden to a doctor's appointment when he was one month old. This was one of the appointments that Desiree absolutely hated because he was getting his first Hepatitis B shot. Please bear in mind that Desiree used to struggle not to cry when Caden was crying because he was sleepy. A shot? Sweet, Holy 7lbs. 8oz., newborn infant Jesus! The world was most certainly coming to an end. After his routine checkup, the doctor said, "Alright, the nurse is going to come in to give little Caden his shot now. He'll only have one today, but next visit he'll get four more." Inquiring as to why my son would have to endure so much agony, I asked, "Doctor, why so many shots?" He responds, "Well, to help his immune system and protect him from dangerous diseases in the long run. It will hurt now, but you'll be glad he went through it in the long run." Then, in came the nurse and out went my wife. Bless her motherly heart. Holding my son and attempting to console him as much as I could, the nurse with this crazed look in her eyes reached back like she was about to pitch a fastball in the major leagues and stabbed my child with a 14-inch needle. Of course, I may have over exaggerated with one or two details, but parents, you know the feeling when your son or daughter is in pain. No matter how old they are, you're in pain, too! To hear my son scream at the top of his lungs as the sound of pain echoed throughout the hospital was simply heartbreaking; but, as his father, I have a responsibility to ensure that he is protected, provided for, and covered; even if that means holding him through painful situations that will help him throughout his life.

It is amazing how much your children will teach you about your Heavenly Father. Many times, purpose and greatness are incubated in the womb of pain. While it may not be favorable to our emotions, it is beneficial for us in the future. There was a woman in the scriptures by the name of Hannah. At the onset of the book of 1 Samuel, we are immediately introduced to the foundation of purposeful pain which is located in a marriage between one man, Elkanah, and two women, Peninnah and Hannah.[13] Don't get too excited now! Jesus believes in monogamy. The challenge that you'll find in this household is that, as the Bible states, Peninnah had children, but Hannah had no children. Why? Because the Lord had shut up her womb. Twenty-first century minds would say, people have challenges with barrenness every day, so that's why there are options like adoption. Consider, Hannah was in a time

---

[13] See "Treasurers in The Word" chapter to read the scripture text in its entirety.

and society where they ascribed the value of a woman to her ability to reproduce. This was not her fault, she did not sin. This was not the devil. God did this. Often times, when our flesh goes before our spirit in our mental state, it will cause us to be spiritually blinded by the burden which results in us attempting to rebuke something that actually originated from God for our benefit.

That's the difference between "divine affliction" and "demonic affliction". The objective of divine affliction, while it may still sting, has a greater goal which is the production of life with purpose. Intentions are not the same when it comes to demonic affliction. The purpose of demonic affliction is rooted in the systematic destruction of your destiny and your life. You see, there are some lessons and levels in God that can only be taught in the school of affliction. While it may be hard to believe, the pain, frustration, and trouble are all a part of the lesson plan. David captured this understanding about Professor Jesus as he shares in Psalm 119:71 KJV[14] *"It is good for me that I have been afflicted; that I might learn thy statutes."* From grade school through college, not one of my teachers or professors gave me their lesson plan. They provided a syllabus, but never the lesson plan. Any teacher will tell you, no lesson plan for any academic year is developed off a whim or at random. Lesson plans, tests, pop-quizzes, and the like are constructed with your development in mind well in advance before the first day of school. I would say the Lord is the same way. In order for you to reach your

---

[14] See "Treasurers in The Word" chapter to read the scripture text in its entirety.

intended purpose, you have to endure the plan. "Well James, this doesn't feel good." It's not about if it "feels good". All "good things" from the Lord don't always "feel good". The objective is not to feel good in it; it's to glory in it. Paul said in 2 Corinthians 12:9-10 KJV[15],

> "[9]Most gladly therefore will I rather glory in my infirmities, that the power of Christ may rest upon me. [10]Therefore I take pleasure in infirmities, in reproaches, in necessities, in persecutions, in distresses for Christ's sake: for when I am weak, then am I strong."

I love this chapter because it shines a light of encouragement on the discouraged, confused, and those in need of direction in dark seasons. The greatest treasure you'll find in this chapter is the purpose of the pain and the glory behind the grief. Go ahead, be encouraged. In the words of my uncle, Bishop J. LaVerne Tyson, "It shall, it shall be well."

***Anyone in your life that causes you
more grief than relief has got to be
released because you can't live in peace
dealing with people who live off drama.***

***Whoever told you you're not good
enough, not smart enough, not pretty
enough, not educated enough, not rich
enough, just put you in the perfect***

---

[15] See "Treasurers in The Word" chapter to read the scripture text in its entirety.

position for God to show them and you that, when He is on your side, you have MORE THAN ENOUGH!!

If you are going to enter into it, you have got to break out of it.

Don't let your pain make you forget God's promises.

Don't let your pain make you panic, because what shall be produced is greater power.

God did not give Job double for his trouble until after Job blessed God, not only for what he gave, but also for what he had taken away. If you can bless God when you have NOTHING, then He knows He can trust you with everything.

Rebuke that lying spirit telling you God has abandoned you! There is NO WAY you would have survived what you've been through if God wasn't on your side. If He brought you through THAT

*He's going to bring you through THIS!
Now you get up and tell the devil you
only have two words to say to him: NO
WEAPON!!*

*The reason why the miracle has not
happened yet is because not enough of
your enemies have arrived yet.*

Be patient. The power is in the process.

*You cannot be powerful until you are
fully acquainted with the word
"painful".*

*God will never allow you to sow more in
sorrow than you reap in joy.*

*I just looked at the schedule and you
have an appointment with JOY in the
morning!*

*My present appearance doesn't show
my past pain.*

Although God has taken from you, God has not forsaken you.

One thing separates a praiser from a worshipper: pain.

Pain is an equal opportunity employer.

You may be broke right now, but God is going to take you to a place of surplus and more than enough.

The things that have caused me the most pain, have developed within me the most power.

When this is over you will say, "It hurt me, but it helped me".

When people intentionally hurt you, they don't realize that they unintentionally help you. Thank all your haters for driving you directly into the LOVE of GOD.

You won't know God until you accept the pain that comes with letting go of that which your heart desires to hold onto the most.

Your heart may be broken in a million pieces, but don't despair because He's taking you from broken PIECES to PERFECT PEACE.

To all my brothers who are hurting, tears are not a sign of weakness. They are a sign of the strength to trust God in the midst of pain beyond words. There is a pain beyond words, but there is no pain that is beyond God's power to heal. So, go ahead and let them see you cry because not many days hence, God is going to let them see you rejoice!

The people that hurt you the most didn't know they were being used by God to help you the most because their divine betrayal taught you not to trust in man and how to trust in God. So, don't hate 'em...thank 'em.

Affliction is not punishment; it is God's Prerequisite for power.

Failure is only fatal if you choose to give up instead of GET UP!

Pain always gives you a clearer perspective of God for who He really is.

Never run from pain. You will never know power until you first, know pain

It is what breaks you that makes you.

Suffering in the Lord doesn't guarantee you won't lose anything; it's quite the opposite. It guarantees you will lose everything, but gain greater.

Do not allow mourning to abort ministry.

God said you have moved from MOURNING to MORNING!

❖ ❖ ❖

Don't retreat, but recover!!

God's purpose involves pain for the perfecting of the saints.

Pain will help you bring spiritual things in their right perspective.

Pain will help you put some of the foolishness out of your life.

The Lord told me to tell you to stop mourning over being rejected by people and start rejoicing over being accepted by GOD.

If you woke up this morning and wished the sun had stayed down, I rebuke the spirit of depression away from you and declare in the name of the Lord Jesus that "THE LIGHT" in your soul will exceed the light in the sky and I declare and decree in the name of Jesus Christ that you shall LIVE and NOT DIE!!

If your past determined your future, you would be dead already. Stop expecting a repeat of what has been and start expecting a RELEASE of that which shall be!

Once you have been knocked down, you will respect the courage it takes to get back up again.

Don't you die now! You've got more living to do!

Your suffering is the most authentic sign of your sonship.

It is not the good times that define a man's character, but it's the bad times.

Good times teach us how good God is, but the bad times teach us how GREAT God is.

Affliction will give you a disposition to pray.

Affliction will help you get your priorities in place.

Pain always produces progress.

Your gain is coming out of your pain. The worst thing that ever happened to you is really the best thing that ever happened to you.

That pain is the source of your power.

Treasure Reflections

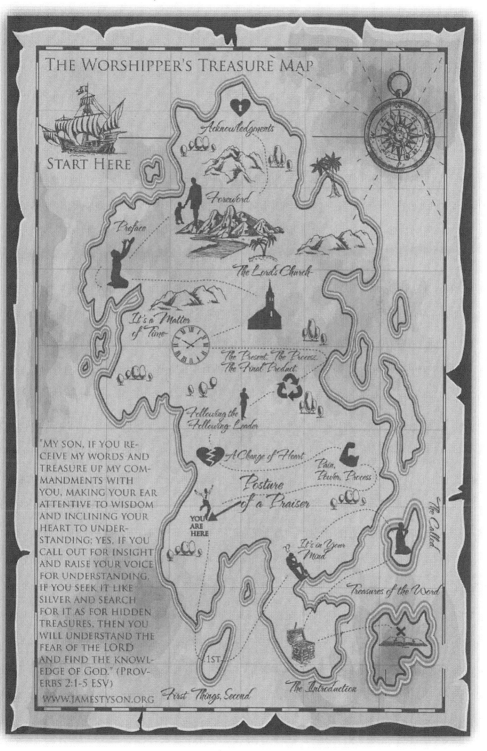

Chapter 7

THE POSTURE OF A PRAISER

An American philosopher and psychologist by the name of William James, stated, "The deepest principle in human nature is the craving to be appreciated." Embedded within the mind and heart of an individual, whether verbally or nonverbally communicated, is a desire to be valued, loved, and appreciated by those within their immediate circle or by other individuals in which he or she has attempted to exemplify kindness, hospitality, and even implement, what we know as, the golden rule that Jesus shares near the end of the Sermon on the Mount. Jesus says in Matthew 7:12 [16], *"Therefore all things whatsoever ye would that men should do to you, do ye even so to them: for this is the law and the prophets."* Here, Jesus brings us to the awareness that our actions, responses, and expressions to/toward others should not be predicated upon the actions of others; however, our actions should be predicated upon the standard of love that we would desire to be reciprocated.

One of my prayers for the past several years now has been, "Lord Jesus, teach me to love how you designed love to be." You see, I had a tendency to love people how I felt

---

[16] See "Treasurers in The Word" chapter to read the scripture text in its entirety.

they should be loved; a lot here, a little here, not at all over there, or absolutely none at all. I think now would be a good time to join me in that same prayer. Before you just repeat these words, I want you to take a moment a read them first, because once you open the door in prayer, you have to walk through it. Only if you want this kind of heart , say this prayer: Lord, help me to see others the way you see them and love them how you love them.

In the study of the power of interpersonal communications, great scholars and researchers suggest that within the first thirty seconds of conversation, one should make an effort to say something that shows that you appreciate and affirm that individual. As a result, you have set the tone of the rest of the conversation because you have given the individual a sense of value. Dr. John C. Maxwell (one of my favorite authors and teachers) stated in his book, *Be A People Person: Effective Leadership Through Effective Relationships*, "Most of us think wonderful things about people, but they never know it. Too many of us tend to be tight-fisted with our praise. It's of no value if all you do is think it; it becomes valuable when you impart it."

While I agree wholeheartedly with the statements of Dr. William James and Dr. Maxwell as it pertains to the development of our personal appreciation, communication, and affirmation of others, one has to consider the heart of God. I have found that this same concept not only applies to our appreciation for one another and our interpersonal communication, but also to the praise of God. Most of us think wonderful things about God, but it never comes out of our mouth. True praise that

TREASURES OF A WORSHIPPER

resides in the heart of an individual is not to be confined nor trapped behind the inner recesses of the mind, and certainly not restrained by one's intellect or sophistication. On the contrary, praise is what I would consider to be "the great equalizer". The scriptures share in Psalm 150:6 KJV[17], *"Let every thing that hath breath praise the Lord. Praise ye the Lord."*

What concerns me is our spiritual understanding of praise, which is clouded by our inaccurate representation of what praise was truly designed to do. Praise was never designed to obtain possessions or to get out of something. To say that praise only pays your light bill is an inaccurate representation of the purpose and power of praise. Before his expulsion from heaven, praise was not just an "it", praise was a "he". When describing Lucifer prior to his expulsion from heaven, the scriptures say, *"...the workmanship of thy tabrets and of thy pipes was prepared in thee in the day that thou wast created."*[18] So, the power harnessed within praise has the potential to do much more than simply cover a car note. Psalm 22:3 KJV says[19], *"But thou art holy, O thou that inhabitest the praises of Israel."* Praise is solely and exclusively designed for ascribing greatness to our God and it is God that inhabits that praise. Remember, praise is not confined to a space or location. So

---

[17] See "Treasurers in The Word" chapter to read the scripture text in its entirety.

[18] See "Treasurers in The Word" chapter to read the scripture text in its entirety.

[19] See "Treasurers in The Word" chapter to read the scripture text in its entirety.

then, if I can get God into a room through my praise, God himself will take care of the need. Do you see it? You just focus on giving Him glory and His presence will take care of everything else.

Understand this principle: Praise is positional and intentional. As a praiser, your posture is always toward HIM and never them or it. Over these few years that I have been in ministry, there have been many occasions, while watching the "praiselessness" of people, where I have wanted to take the microphone and toss it into the congregation, grab and chop up every pew into little toothpicks, set them on fire, and scream at the top of my lungs. It's challenging looking at people, to whom you know God has been nothing but good, sit as if they've never experienced an ounce of grace or mercy. Talk about frustration! This is where positional and intentional praise takes precedence. When you are focused on the presence of the Lord and not the response of the people, atmospheres shift. Whether you are a pastor, worship leader, or a member who attends regularly, everyone can fall victim to the spirit of Michal, David's wife (See 2 Samuel 6).[20]. The scriptures share that when David was bringing in the Ark of the Covenant into the City of David with dancing and rejoicing, his wife, Michal *"looked through a window, and saw king David leaping and dancing before the Lord; and she despised him in her heart."* The key is how you respond to the opposing forces of praise. Had David allowed himself to be consumed by Michal's lack of

---

[20] See "Treasurers in The Word" chapter to read the scripture text in its entirety.

worship and her negative sarcasm, it could have prevented him from being blessed just like her. David had a level of determination in praise that was not driven nor moved by his environment; he created the environment wherever he went.

As you focus your mind on the treasures of praise, take a moment to evaluate your praise to your God. Has it been persuaded by others' opinions or actions? Do you praise out of ritual and not by the request of God? Do you have the proper posture of a praiser? Let's find out!

While there is a void, there is no blood. While it's missing, there is no massacre. Things aren't as bad as they could be and it could be worse. But God is just allowing it to be hid until your praise finds it.

You don't have a bill that praise can't pay.

Your praise will not only deliver you, but it will deliver those who are not aware of the principles of praise, but need to be delivered by them.

Sinners reserve the option, when or if they will bless God's name. But you're not in that number! Despite what type

of week you have had, God is still worthy of all praise!

Your unusual praises will change your status from delayed to delivered.

Your praise cannot be so little for blessings so big.

Your praise affects my future.

You can never praise God too much, but you can praise Him too little.

I can praise God with you, but I cannot praise Him for you.

Praise is not based on external motivation.

When pain is not balanced out with praise, frustration with people will result in ingratitude towards God.

I will no longer live from paycheck to paycheck, but from praise to praise.

There is a whole dimension of God that can only be revealed through tear stained praises.

God never answers prayers until you praise Him.

It is the combination of prayer and praise that produces perfect peace.

There's more than one way to lie. You can lie with your mouth and you can lie with your actions. Whenever you sit in God's house praiseless, you're a liar.

All praises are not created equal. All praisers are created equal.

All praises do not possess the same power because they do not all share the same value.

Stop worrying about questions that don't have answers and praise God for the answers that have no questions.

Praise will take you into a dimension where you can get your needs met.

You never want to sit out on a time of praise, because you never know which praise is going to unlock heaven over your head.

Make your praise proactive. Why? Because the way God is getting ready to bless you, you're going to have to get an early start for the blessings that are getting ready to overtake you.

Because you are a praiser, the devil can steal from you, but he can't kill you.

Send your praise where your pain is not able to go.

*Stop trying to pay your way out of debt.
Praise your way out of debt.*

*Learn to give God praise for the
progress you have made in the process
of growth and development in God.
Don't despise your process.*

*Please don't think that anyone in the
church has a right to determine how
you praise God.*

*Your praise will sustain you until
sunrise.*

*Praise will give you peace in the rough
places.*

Your praise keeps you dreaming.

*Praise increases spiritual perception of
unlimited possibilities.*

Praise is not an end to itself, but it's a means to an end.

One thing an out of season praiser must learn is how to praise God for your own survival.

The week I have had will not determine the praise I give God today.

When you have the discipline to praise God at all times, your environment won't change you, you'll change your environment.

Impose your spiritual influence in every natural and spiritual environment.

Praise creates faith.

If you give God what He wants He will give you everything you need.

Our persuasion is what causes us to maintain our praise in times like these.

If you want your praise to really work on Sunday you've got to learn how to praise Him somewhere else besides the sanctuary.

It is praise that puts revelation in motion for the sake of impartation.

When preaching pauses, praise must continue.

Never allow the enemy to make you ignore the priority of your praise.

My praise not only determines whether I live or die, but it determines how I live or die.

Your praise affects the quality of your life.

Praise makes you beautiful to God.

Here's a reason to give God praise: It's going to happen!

An ugly praise will release a beautiful miracle!

Without praise you can observe the principles, patterns, pretenses and protocol of God, but you cannot access the presence of God.

Your praise makes a difference in the atmosphere. When you sit in a worship service and hold back your praise, you are holding back someone else deliverance. Your praise IS the difference between life and death for someone's soul.

Treasure Reflections

_____

_____

_____

_____

_____

_____

_____

_____

_____

_____

_____

_____

_____

_____

_____

_____

_____

_____

_____

_____

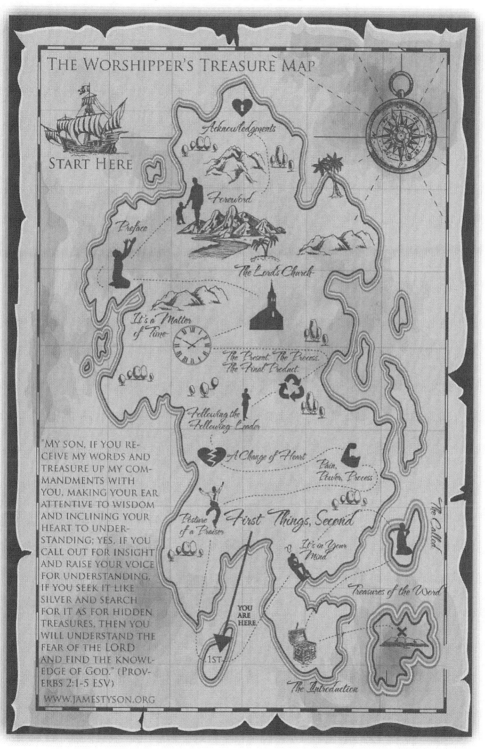

Chapter 8

FIRST THINGS, SECOND

Eric Fromm, a German psychologist, stated, "To love somebody is not just a strong feeling-it is a decision, it is a judgment, it is a promise." There is an intentional expression of time, thought, energy, and passion that is exemplified from an individual that has prioritized their value to/toward another. There is just no getting around it. When you truly love something or someone you deliberately prioritize them in your life. There is absolutely nothing on this Earth that will take precedence over my family. Why? Because of the value I ascribe to them. When you consider it, the quality of every person's life is embedded, not within materialistic possessions, but rather within a person's intangible core values. What an individual ascribes value to, governs their actions, thought patterns, and even their approach to spiritual things. Consider the antithesis: if something is of no value to you, your time, thoughts, and energy become extremely scarce because this matter, topic, or person holds no special significance to your life. Jesus said, as He is teaching His disciples, in Luke 12:34 KJV[21], *"For where your treasure is, there will your heart be also."*

---

[21] See "Treasurers in The Word" chapter to read the scripture text in its entirety.

Within the values of each individual is a common denominator and that is the heart. The expression of what we value is governed by the heart. The heart puts a demand upon a corresponding action. If it is truly in my heart, in some way, it will be expressed either in my speech, day-to-day actions, or the lack thereof. I'm going to ask you a question, but before you respond, think. How do you value your relationship with God and how do you express to Him the value you ascribe to your relationship? Does it show in your prayer life, in your worship, or personal devotional with the Lord? One of my most intimate concerns as I travel, that I often bring before the Lord in prayer, is the lack of spiritual value that we place upon our relationship with the Lord. Our materialistic driven society has created an epidemic within the Christian community, where there is much more appreciation for the things of God, than for God himself. In short, we have placed "first things, second."

Jesus says in Matthew 6:33 KJV[22], *"But seek ye first the kingdom of God, and his righteousness; and all these things shall be added unto you."* Whenever your values are properly prioritized, meaning you have placed God as #1 in your life, you have placed yourself on the side of the advantage. I have always been fascinated by this scripture, not for "the things", but for the acquisition of the Kingdom of God and His righteousness. There is an intentional undertone when Jesus says that things shall be "added", but not "given". Whenever something is given, you have the choice to accept whether you want to take it or not, but

---

[22] See "Treasurers in The Word" chapter to read the scripture text in its entirety.

when it is "added", something is joined, put in, or mixed together so as to increase the size, number, or amount. There is a wholeness that is obtained when the center of your priorities are upon the Lord; however, the pursuit of God is so powerful that it creates a supernatural magnetic attraction for increase. Here's the key we have to comprehend: even if the increase was not promised, God is still the ultimate reward. Notice, Jesus never says, "I'm bringing the addition with me." No, it's being added to YOU. What significance does that have for us? That means, when you ascribe enough value to God to make Him first in your pursuit, when you seek Him and find Him, there is completeness in Him that nothing else can fill. When you are in Him, the things are added to YOU. This means that whatever is connected to you, as a result of you being engulfed in Him, must be increased. How can God be increased when He is already complete? He can't! He's already perfect. It has to be added to YOU. I hope you can see how much of a blessing it is to make God first in your life!

Let's look at it this way. Say the Lord blesses you with a wonderful job paying a substantial amount of money per year, which allows you to meet all of your financial obligations, tithes and offerings, and have something left over for savings and recreation. Wouldn't that be a great? With this job comes full benefits that are added to you, which affect other areas of your life because you have the job. Do you see it? The same principle is applicable in making God your "first thing". As you discover the treasure of prioritizing the presence of God in your life, I want you to consider who or what you have you replaced God with in your life. Is it friends, money, your career, your spouse? Let's make God first again!

The only thing sweeter than experiencing the presence of God is experiencing it again.

Sin is never your friend. It not only separates you from the presence of God.

God will not allow Satan to give you more in sin than He will give you in righteousness.

Instead of working to live we should be living to worship.

Soul saving first begins with soul seeking, followed by soul winning.

I will be faithful to my promise, my covenant, and my God!

The grace of God will never fail a man, but a man can fail the grace of God.

I wonder if God's feelings get hurt when we say we are lonely and He's been waiting for us to talk to Him all day.

God is real! But you will never know it if you only interact with fake church folk.

Don't let church make you lose your soul. Religion will kill you, but Jesus will heal you.

You will never have spiritual understanding if you are attempting to understand God from a human point of view.

Whenever you want to find your identity, read the bible.

Move from relationship [with God] to revelation of God.

There is a difference and distinction between those who go to church and those who go to worship.

God will do anything for you if you keep Him first, but God will do nothing for you if you make Him second.

Your relationship with God is not based upon your denomination or organizational affiliation because there are those who have come to the house of God all their life, but don't know God.

You cannot determine salvation by one's outward appearance, but it must be determined by their fruit.

There is a critical difference between a Christian and a church member.

Religious people's prayers are self-centered and focused toward their desires and not God's desires.

Spiritual worship is centered, not on what I want, but what God desires.

The best way to start the day is to PRAY!

Where we sit spiritually will determine whether we move forward or stay still.

In order to seek the kingdom, you must first seek the King of the kingdom.

Get to a place in God where you never fail or are never defeated.

Until you are willing to give God all of you, God cannot give your ministry, or YOU, all of Him.

You cannot keep a part of yourself to yourself and expect God to use you completely.

Consecration does not deal with sin,
but it deals with self.

Realign yourself with purpose.

Reestablish your consistency.

When you abide in the shadow at all
times God will abide in your shadow.

There is nothing common about the
uncommon power of the Holy Ghost in
your spirit.

Your spirituality is based on how you
treat those that hate you.

What the word of God will do for you
depends on what you will do with it.

The devil will always recognize a
worshipper.

A perplexed life becomes your daily reality when you read the bible with your eyes wide shut and if you read it from the perspective of presumption and not expectation.

The pursuit of knowledge that excludes God always ends in foolishness.

Being saved is neither a sprint nor a relay race, but you can consider it as a cross country event. If you try to get somewhere in God too fast you will become weary in well doing.

Whatever you prioritize you will pursue.

If you follow Jesus, you can expect a cross.

If you do not follow Him, you cannot be like Him.

There is no way a human mind can comprehend the mind or the intellect of God.

The purpose of God always takes precedence over the presence of God; meaning, just because you can get God where you want Him to be, doesn't always mean He's going to do what you tell Him to do.

The presence of God must be pursued in order to be possessed.

Holiness will bring about whole-ness.

Enough time in the word will make a mean man a sweet man.

Manifest power is always the end result of properly managed priorities.

We must recommit to reading our word because God may not be saying this time, what He said last time.

God has used imperfect situations to prepare you for perfect promises.

When you really love God, there are some things you just won't do!

God does things for worshippers that He doesn't do for spectators.

Treasure Reflections

Chapter 9

IT'S IN YOUR MIND

Growing up, I suffered the blessing of being an only child. Those with multiple siblings could not relate to the previous statement. There were days (excluding birthdays, holidays, and special events) where I wished I had biological siblings to talk to, build relationship with, and blame things on. It was awfully challenging to find someone to blame, when I made the conscious decision to cut my own hair at around ten years old. That's another story for another day, but the moral of the story is "Available clippers + curious child = a race track down the middle of your head and an awkward Nike sign on the side". Let's just say it ended catastrophically. Nevertheless, I did have the benefit of having cousins around my age, which didn't make my life as an only child too bad. I remember my cousins, Justin and Chandice, would often spend the night at our house growing up. They spent more time at our house than I did at theirs because, in the middle of the night, I would disappear without a trace. What really happened is that I called my mother to come pick me up because I didn't want to be there anymore. We spent so much time together that you would've thought we were siblings.

Chandice would sleep in the guest room while Justin and I would sleep in my room and play on my PlayStation most of the night. However, Justin had a tremendous challenge with staying in my room because he was subject to my worst enemy, the dark. Oh, I hated and feared the dark! So much so, that I had a 4-foot-tall, bright orange, jack o'lantern as my night light. That thing was just as bright as turning on the actual room light. Justin despised that big'ol pumpkin! For the sake of not being offensive, I will not disclose the harsh words I endured each and every night he slept on the floor in my room. I had to fall asleep with it on, it had to be on while I was sleep, and if you unplugged it, I knew it. He just didn't understand that the jack o'lantern was my safe place. He would tell me, "Jamie, it's just as dark when you close your eyes! Turn this thing off! It's all in your mind, man." I didn't care what he said, but, I suppose he was right. The inward fear I had of the dark, in my mind, was projected through outwardly through my actions, so much so, that I inflicted my mind's reality upon others.

It is absolutely remarkable how your mind, or a single thought, can have an impact on your life. The mind is the ultimate battleground where wars are won or lost, before they ever physically manifest themselves. Just like when I was a child, the darkness of the mind is far more daunting than what we actually see. How we govern our thoughts plays a tremendous role in life. What you will discover, like the impotent man at the pool of Bethesda in John 5:1-9[23], is that the impotency in your actions is not the root of the problem. The impotency of your mind is the source of your limitations and your inability to be

---

[23] See "Treasurers in The Word" chapter to read the scripture text in its entirety.

everything God has destined you to be. Former President Franklin D. Roosevelt once said, "The only limit to our realization of tomorrow will be our doubts of today." I could not think of a truer statement. Proverbs 23:7 KJV[24] says it this way, *"For as he thinketh in his heart, so is he: Eat and drink, saith he to thee; but his heart is not with thee."* Who I am today is a product of what I thought or presently think about myself.

When you see the word "thinketh" in the above scripture, it does not refer to one singular thought. Rather, it refers to your limitless living in Christ being birthed from the evolution of your thinking. In short, it is what I like to call progressive thought. Often times, I try to encourage those I speak with concerning destiny or personal challenges by sharing with them that just because you thought "limited" about yourself one day, doesn't mean you have to continue thinking that way. It is easy to become discouraged when you make strides to overcome the dark, but you still feel as if you need the nightlight. Do not be ashamed to live positively one thought at a time. Press toward God's thoughts.

One of the challenges that very critical people have (and I am one of them) is the expectation of thinking about oneself the way God thinks about us overnight. The reality is that God has been thinking the same way about you before you were ever formed in your mother's womb. My life in Him is spent trying to catch up to His thinking! If you really think about it, it's going to take you an entire lifetime

---

[24] See "Treasurers in The Word" chapter to read the scripture text in its entirety.

to try to catch up to God's thoughts about you. As soon as you capture a thought, embrace it! Take a moment, and encourage yourself to think again.

The problem is not what people say about you, it's what you *think* about what they say about you. My happiness or sadness, my success or failure, my peace or perplexity is a product or the poverty of my own thoughts. So, to think limitlessly, you must think with the mind of Christ. Philippians 2:5 KJV[25] says it this way, *"Let this mind be in you, which was also in Christ Jesus..."* It really is all in your mind! As you are discovering the treasures of thought, allow the framework of your mind to be restructured so you can be who you already are in God's mind. Remember, you are what you think.

> **The secret to successful living can be understood through how God thinks and what He thinks about me.**

> **You will always be frustrated with God if you continue to compare your thoughts to God's thoughts when we don't think like Him.**

> **You never have to worry about God making a mistake!**

---

[25] See "Treasurers in The Word" chapter to read the scripture text in its entirety.

The mind, itself, is the greatest agent of worship.

You cannot live with an old mind in a new season.

Don't doubt what God has said because of what you don't see!

When you walk with God long enough, your history will help you not question God's motives. If He did it before, He can do it again.

When you purify your environment, you will purify your mind.

Whenever you get to the place where you think you know more than God, you have reduced yourself to the status of a fool.

In some people's attempt to show you how much they know, they end up

showing you how much they don't know.

Distraction leads to destruction.

Unless you are willing to rethink God and see Him for who He really is, you will never become who you really are!

You are measured by the quality of your thinking.

A kingdom minded minister is not worried about the poverty of the place, but he/she is concerned with the wealth of the people.

A secular mind with no spiritual influence is a savage.

A transformed mind will always keep you living outside the lines of limitations.

You cannot change your behavior until you change your mind.

The first person that hears the negative words that come out of your mouth is you. Your mind hears those negative words before you do.

Stop trying to interpret spiritual things with your natural mind.

You can never accomplish the will of God with a fearful mind.

In order to get on God's mind, you must change your mind.

In order to get to 100%, you must position your mind in worship.

The management of our minds, in our house, affects the effect of worship in God's house.

Effective worship deals with the state of mind.

You don't pray to change God's mind, you pray and God changes your mind.

The people that think they know you the most are the ones that know you the least.

If the preachers don't know who God is, the people will never hear who He is.

There is no conflict between knowledge and power because when you have power, but no knowledge, you become destructive and not constructive.

Knowing about Jesus is not better than knowing Jesus.

The lack of knowledge, as it relates to God's word, has a direct correlation to one's perception of self, one's perception of others, one's perception

*of God, and one's quality or lack of
quality of life.*

*Education helps you understand what
you don't know. It is a lifelong process.*

*Wisdom is the systematic application
of real life situations that have been
acquired through the pursuit of
knowledge.*

*God does not judge a person for what
he/she does not know, but what he/she
does know, but will refuse to do.*

*You cannot conquer what you will not
confront.*

*Before you can stabilize your life,
finances, career, and family, you must
stabilize your mind.*

*Just because people think you are a
genius, does not mean that God does
not know you are dummy.*

There are people who can control the civilized world if they can control their uncivilized mouth.

You will only be as great as you say you will be.

Your words control your feelings.

Every child of God must know how to operate in two worlds without compromising the integrity of the Holy Ghost.

The same attitude you have when you look in the mirror is the same attitude you should have when you look into the word.

Do not feel the word, think the word.

The only way the enemy can prevent what God showed you will come into

manifestation, is to get you to doubt what He said.

If vision is to become a reality, you must believe with your whole heart what God said.

The lack of focus will create instability in every area of your life.

You will never fulfill purpose, even if you are full of power, if you don't have the patience to wait on the Lord.

God wants you to change your focus from the way you see things to the way God's said things.

You must search the scripture for the knowledge to achieve understanding.

Treasure Reflections

_____

_____

_____

_____

_____

_____

_____

_____

_____

_____

_____

_____

_____

_____

_____

_____

_____

_____

_____

_____

_____

_____

Chapter 10

At the age of 13, I humbly answered the call of God to the ministry and to carry this great Gospel to whomever and wherever there was a soul in need of the transformative power of Jesus Christ. The method the Lord used to call me was very similar to the prophet Samuel. Three times young Samuel went to Eli, the priest, with the assumption that he was calling Samuel's name. Finally, on the fourth call, Eli gave Samuel directives that were necessary to launch him from being called to answering the calling of God. This was almost identical to the times I would shout from my room, "Yes sir!", because I was under the impression that it was my father calling me, when it was actually my Heavenly Father.

Upon answering the call to the ministry, I spoke with my parents as well as our pastor (my grandfather), the early and great Bishop James E. Tyson, to inform them of what I felt so strongly in my spirit. At that time, when you shared with the Bishop your call to the ministry, he did not give you your minister's license, a clergy collar, and a microphone and thrust you out onto the public platform to preach. Instead of him giving you a Bible, he would give you a big broom and all 15 of his books to carry wherever he so desired.

A few months or years would go by and you would eventually be elevated to the "Scrape and Scrub Ministry" where you would have extreme privilege to work with Elder Sora Walker, scraping all the gum from under the pews and scrubbing the toilets. It was your job to ensure the house of God remained beautified for God and the people of God. A few more months or years would go by and then you would get another elevation to become the honorable grass cutter, hedges trimmer, and official painter of Christ Church Apostolic. After a few years of preaching to yourself on a ladder or under a pew, instead of calling the pastor "Bishop", you might be tempted to call him "Bishop Pharaoh". I did not understand it then, but now I appreciate my grandfather and my father for teaching me the art of true servanthood.

Jesus shares with the multitude in Matthew 23:11-12 KJV[26], *"11But he that is greatest among you shall be your servant. 12And whosoever shall exalt himself shall be abased; and he that shall humble himself shall be exalted."* Looking at the climate of churches, mainstream ministries, and the body of Christ at large, it would appear that these words of Jesus have been deleted from the holy word of God. Now, everybody wants a title, a position, and seventeen armor bearers, but will refuse pick up the fans off the pews after the worship service because, "that's not my job". Might I share with you a lesson I had to learn early in ministry? If you are going to be in the service of the Lord, humility is not a request, it is a mandate.

---

[26] See "Treasurers in The Word" chapter to read the scripture text in its entirety.

When servitude has died in you, pride sets in like rigor mortise. When rigor mortise sets in, it does not take long (studies suggest two to six hours) for your body to become stiff. Your desires to serve others, vision, passion to feed the homeless, develop programming for delivered and recovering addicts, and your heart for ministry stiffens when it is infected with pride. You remember in 2 Chronicles 26[27], when Uzziah became the King of Judah, he started off his administration the right way because the scriptures teach us he did what was pleasing in the sight of God; however, when he became strong, his heart was lifted up to his destruction. Because the Lord hates pride, to humble him, He struck him with leprosy.

As the called of God, there are two key things you must have: humility and identity. As I shared in the previous chapters, one of the greatest tragedies any individual could ever experience is to live an entire lifetime and not know themselves one day. For years, people become successful representatives of themselves, without activating their authentic selves, because they are afraid of what is behind the door of destiny. My friend, the world can't wait anymore for you to be you. Average and mediocrity will always be the enemies of your destiny. The challenge individuals have is that when they get the call of God, they want to choose the occupation and choose it on their own time. You cannot be everything that God wants you to be until you learn to give up everything you want to be. If you attempt to conceptualize what you want to be in

---

[27] See "Treasurers in The Word" chapter to read the scripture text in its entirety.

ministry without the consultation of God, you will always live beneath your privileges and power.

When you say that you want to be used in the ministry, what you are truly saying is, "I want to be a servant"; but what must be deciphered is, "in what capacity am I called to serve?" What's worse than not operating in your calling is operating in the wrong calling. In many ministries, globally, there is poor "purpose placement" from those in leadership, for those operating in various areas of the ministries. For example, just because someone has a desire to sing does not mean that the Lord has called them to be the praise and worship leader. Similarly, just because someone is an administrator in their secular profession, does not mean that God has called them to administrate in the Kingdom. Just because someone is good at a trade does not license them to practice that trade in the Kingdom. There must be appropriate "purpose placement". What has God invested in you to do in the Kingdom? Being good at it and called to it are two different areas of focus.

I use the word "kingdom" purposefully because the call of God may not always be within the four walls of a church. You must see that! It can easily become frustrating when you feel like you do not fit into an "auxiliary" or "ministry", and that leads to the feeling of, "there's nothing in church for me to do". This could be far beyond the truth! Your focus must be, "Lord, what is it, and where are you placing me for your service?"

There are three things that most people get confused when seeking God for what capacity they are supposed to operate in: their talent, their gift, and their calling. Most do not know that there is a difference between them. A talent is an ability that can be done, controlled, or developed on your own. A gift is something you are particularly anointed to do; it is an ability from God that cannot be accomplished any other way than with God's help. A calling is a strong inner impulse toward a particular course of action, especially when accompanied by conviction or divine influence. It's a particular task or function God has anointed you to fulfill.

As it pertains to callings, it is possible to operate a talent or a gift, but not be called to do that particular function; however, it is impossible to operate in your calling and not be gifted to do it. A talent is a natural function, but gifts and callings are spiritual functions. In order to operate effectively in your calling, there must be proper management of your gifts. If you mismanage your gifts, your calling will be mismanaged. You must be able to identify one thing: is THIS GIFT for MY CALLING? The scriptures share in 1 Corinthians 12:4,7-12 KJV[28] *"4Now there are diversities of gifts, but the same Spirit."* Meaning, God has intentionally established divine diversification to bring wholeness to the body of Christ. Kingdom impact will be rendered ineffective if it is confined to merely one region of gifts and callings. The deliberate expansion of gifts originating from the same spirit is the strategy of God for the Kingdom citizens to turn the world right side up.

Out of the eleven chapters in this book, I took the most time to talk about and bring understanding to the calling of God. One of the saddest misconceptions that is

---

[28] See "Treasurers in The Word" chapter to read the scripture text in its entirety.

ever so prevalent is when someone says or hears that there is a call upon the life of individual, by default, they are categorized as "preachers". The body of Christ does not lack or have a shortage of preachers by any means. Some who claim to be preachers are merely impressive imposters with great stage presence. They are effective at putting on a production, yet lack the authentic anointing of God; talented, but not anointed. In reality, not everyone is called to the preaching ministry, but everyone is called to be a minister. The true essence of the call of God is to be a minister or servant unto Him and those who you have been called to reach. So, while you may believe it or not, you are the called of God! Yes, you!

As you approach the treasures of the calling of God, I challenge you to seek the Lord concerning the calling on your life. Here's what I want you to be comfortable with. Your calling may not be "the normal". God did not call you to be normal. There's a business that needs your influence, a fashion industry that needs your designs, a sports arena that needs your presence, a stage that needs your artistic creativity, a studio that needs your musical gift and sound. The Lord did not make a mistake when He called you. Embrace the uniqueness of your calling and fulfill it unapologetically.

Do not preach to people that you are not willing to embrace.

When a person is already spiritually unconscious, your preaching will not

bring them back to life. Only God's power can bring a person back to life.

Do not just preach to the people, but reach the people.

When ministers become more interested in being celebrities than servants, the mission loses its integrity. Do it for GOD. Not for gold.

When you are chosen by God, you don't have the luxury of acting your age. You have the responsibility to act your identity.

I'm scared of ministers who love to preach, but hate to pray.

Don't be so concerned about preaching that you forget about lifting the name of Jesus.

You know when you're ready for ministry, when people become more important than popularity.

How many people have lost their souls while we're in pulpits and not on street corners?

You'll never be and become all that God has called you to be until you learn how to value yourself.

It's not always how large is your platform, but it's how large is your influence.

Reaching 1 soul by touching them is more important than preaching a good sermon to 10,000.

PREACHERS: "Your preaching tomorrow will only be as powerful as your prayer tonight"!

Witnessing is our work. Preaching is our privilege.

Your gifting does not reserve you the right not to live a sanctified life.

The chosen have no choice. God has made a decision concerning your destiny and His decision is "victory". Not because of you, but in spite of you.

Whatever it is that is tempting you, it is not worth your anointing or God's favor over your life.

The most essential component of your greatness is patience.

You were chosen to be afflicted because you were chosen to be anointed.

You may not go everywhere to preach, but you must go anywhere God sends you.

*You cannot minister in His presence
and live out of His presence.*

*Great anointing requires great
accountability.*

*Be careful about what you receive into
your spirit by a pessimistic person.*

*Stop trying to prove to people what God
is going to prove to people.*

*Do not forsake doing the right thing in
order to pursue a course of action that
will compromise or jeopardize your
destiny, because you are frustrated
where you are.*

*When you are in route to destiny,
you've got to tell people, "Call me who I
am, not who I was!"*

*Make people respect your atmosphere!
Don't allow people to bring dirty
speaking into your clean atmosphere.*

The greatest sin against God is to say, "I can't" when God said, "You can!"

God is depending on you to be great.

If you are trying to help other people get to heaven, be prepared to go through hell.

God has not prepared you to be a "one hit wonder", but is preparing you for permanent prosperity.

You cannot survive spiritually eating [the word of God] once a week.

Until you're able to handle being alone, you'll never be able to handle being anointed.

There's no group package for the anointing. You've got to get it by yourself.

When you are born again, you are a new creature, but not a perfect creature. You must be matriculated through God ordained pain to reach God's perfection.

I am who I am, but I'm becoming who I shall be.

We have thoughts, feelings, and desires that conflict with God's Word; not because we are not saved, but because we are human. As long as we are in the flesh, evil will be present WITH us, but as long as we are led by the SPIRIT, light will be present IN us. When the flesh is pulling you in the opposite direction of your destiny, LEAN toward the light.

Some nights, prayer is more important than sleep.

The call to lead does not eliminate the necessity to follow.

Sometimes you have to pray all night so you can stay saved all day.

You cannot call yourself saved if you speak in tongues, but won't speak to me.

Purpose is fulfilled within the framework of a preordained path that God has already mapped out in His mind and His thoughts. And those thoughts concerning me take precedent over what I have become in time.

God does more with your destiny in private than He does in public.

You cannot do another man's mission without his mantle.

When you get up to minister, you speak to the people for God, but the worshipper speaks to God.

*You give up all your civilian rights
when you accept the call to ministry.*

A minister is a trustee of truth.

*Maintain holiness and not mainstream
mediocrity.*

A life with Jesus is the best life!

Treasure Reflections

_____

_____

_____

_____

_____

_____

_____

_____

_____

_____

_____

_____

_____

_____

_____

_____

_____

_____

_____

_____

_____

_____

_____

_____

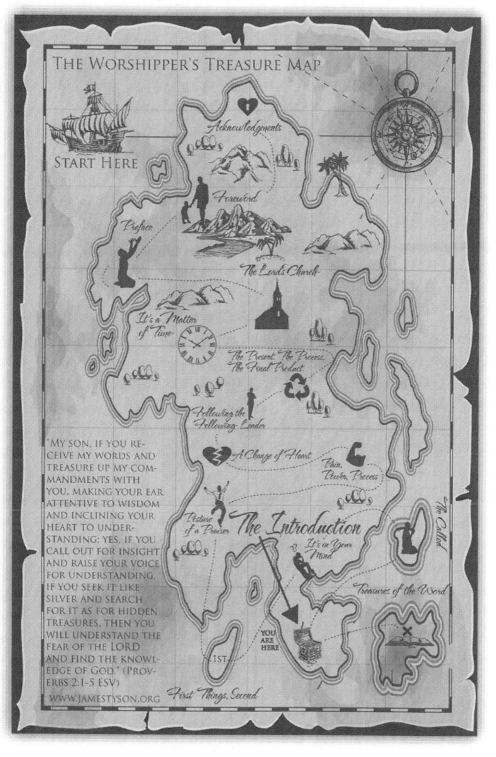

Chapter 11

For decades, historians and treasure hunters have endeavored to discover some of the greatest artifacts, gifts, and invaluable objects that have been produced on the Earth. Remarkable, quite actually, how time and the present echo the same sentiments about its treasure hunters. Buried treasure is one of those things that sound like it only exists in stories. Truthfully, as a child, treasure was only associated with pirates. But what I have come to find in my studies and exposure is that exploration and uncovering of hidden treasurers are merely the surface for those with a heart for this profession. Men such as Captain Martin Bayerle (discovered RMS Republic in 1981), John Mattera (discovered the Golden Fleece, the ship of Joseph Bannister), and E. Lee Spence (discoverer of the Hunley) all shared the common joy of what cannot adequately be described when making a discovery. The joy of the journey, the perseverance in the midst of extreme adversity, and the feeling of accomplishment, along with the responsibility of preservation, all are written between the lines of a treasure hunter's job description.

In 1985, the Polish town of Sroda Slaska was engaged in a renovation process to come of its aged buildings.[29] During the demolition of one of the buildings, a vase was found beneath the foundation. It is said that inside that vase were more than 3,000 silver coins dating back to

---

[29] Dobbs, Sarah. "7 of the Biggest Treasure Troves Ever Found." *Mental Floss*. Mental Floss UK, 24 Mar. 2017. Web. 09 May 2017.

the 14th century. Bear in mind, the era from the 14th century to the 16th century was said to be one of the greatest eras for Poland. Its development as a strong, unified state, territory expansion under Kazimierz the Great, and law/administration reform, all represented the power of Poland during the 14th century. So, what was discovered were not simply coins, but pieces history that connected them to their greatness.

Interestingly enough, that wasn't the conclusion of their findings. A few years later, while continuing town renovations during the demolition of another building nearby, more artifacts were discovered; these findings included a gold crown and a ring bearing the head of a dragon. The value of this new discovery? Approximately $120 million. Millions of dollars worth of history, prestige, and representations of authority were buried beneath the feet of men and women, waiting to be discovered. Here's the key: something (the building, structure, and present occupancy) had to be demolished to get to it.

Out of the numerous stories that could be told concerning hidden treasures, here's the secret to their authenticity. The monetary value (which could range from pennies to millions) holds no comparison to the connection between that treasure and the person or story. "What do you mean, James?" A crown can be sold, but the greatness and history which that crown represents is priceless.

While you have come to the conclusion of *Treasurers of a Worshipper*, you are left with a challenge. The secret to the authenticity of this book is not found in how quickly you read through it or even how much you paid for it. The true worth is what the treasures found within the covers will connect you to after the final period. Time and time again, like me, you will find yourself referring back to these priceless gems. Whether it is just for simple word of encouragement or to receive direction during a very pivotal milestone in your life, you will discover that these are the types of treasures that you keep on discovering. That is the amazing thing about being exposed to wisdom. She will never run out of things to discover about her. The determining factor of the type of impact she will leave upon your life will depend upon how you treasure her. No matter how you turn it or what angle you view it from, wisdom will leave an impact.

I can't tell you enough how much I appreciate you for coming on this journey with me. I encourage you to allow these treasures to be shared and found for the generations to come. Though this is the concluding chapter, you may be wondering why this chapter is entitled, "The Introduction". You see, true seekers of wisdom are not confined nor satisfied at the conclusion of one journey. Why? Because wisdom always leads to the introduction of greater understanding. To my fellow hunter, pursuer, and seeker, your final challenge:

Keep digging.

Final Thoughts

_____

_____

_____

_____

_____

_____

_____

_____

**What was your greatest discovery while reading
Treasures of a Worshipper?**

_____

_____

_____

_____

_____

_____

_____

_____

How will you use these treasures in your life? In what specific areas of your life?

_____

_____

_____

_____

_____

_____

_____

_____

_____

_____

_____

_____

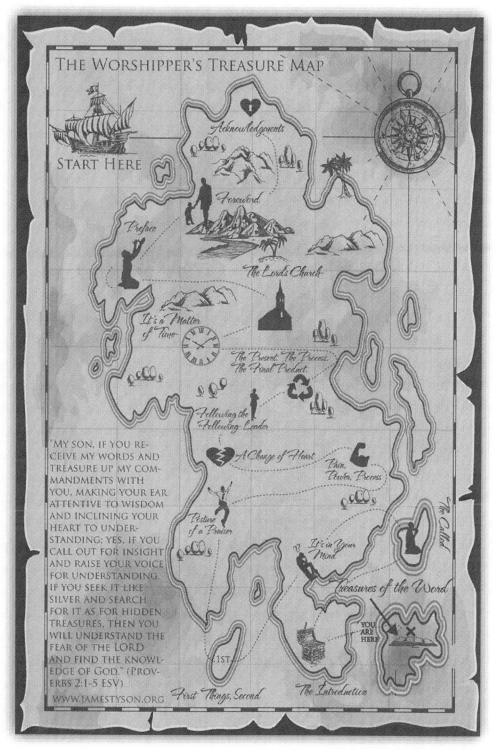

TREASURES OF THE WORD

SCRIPTURE REFERENCES

Everyone does not always have the luxury or privilege of carrying their Bible consistently to search or reference scriptures for a particular point. I understand how difficult it can be sometimes, to have the desire to pull out your Bible and read passages referenced by an author, but circumstances won't allow you to do so. For that reason, below, I have provided each scripture passage referenced in this book. While I do encourage you to study other versions of the Holy Writ, all scriptures provided, unless specified otherwise, are from the King James Version of the Bible.

1. **Joshua 6:1-2,10 KJV**
    [1] Now Jericho was straitly shut up because of the children of Israel: none went out, and none came in. [2] And the Lord said unto Joshua, See, I have given into thine hand Jericho, and the king thereof, and the mighty men of valour. [10] And Joshua had commanded the people, saying, Ye shall not shout, nor make any noise with your voice, neither shall any word proceed out of your mouth, until the day I bid you shout; then shall ye shout.

2. **Proverbs 2:1-5 KJV**
    [1] My son, if thou wilt receive my words, and hide

my commandments with thee; [2] So that thou incline thine ear unto wisdom, and apply thine heart to understanding; [3] Yea, if thou criest after knowledge, and liftest up thy voice for understanding; [4] If thou seekest her as silver, and searchest for her as for hid treasures; [5] Then shalt thou understand the fear of the Lord, and find the knowledge of God.

3. **Matthew 16:16-19 KJV**
[16] And Simon Peter answered and said, Thou art the Christ, the Son of the living God. [17] And Jesus answered and said unto him, Blessed art thou, Simon Bar-jona: for flesh and blood hath not revealed it unto thee, but my Father which is in heaven. [18] And I say also unto thee, That thou art Peter, and upon this rock I will build my church; and the gates of hell shall not prevail against it. [19] And I will give unto thee the keys of the kingdom of heaven: and whatsoever thou shalt bind on earth shall be bound in heaven: and whatsoever thou shalt loose on earth shall be loosed in heaven.

4. **Ecclesiastes 3:1-8 KJV**
[1] To every thing there is a season, and a time to every purpose under the heaven: [2] A time to be born, and a time to die; a time to plant, and a time to pluck up that which is planted; [3] A time to kill, and a time to heal; a time to break down, and a time to build up; [4] A time to weep, and a time to laugh; a time to mourn, and a time to dance; [5] A time to cast away stones, and a time to gather stones together; a time to embrace, and a time to refrain from embracing; [6] A time to get, and a time to lose; a time to keep, and a time to cast away; [7] A time to rend, and a time to sew; a time to keep silence, and a

time to speak; [8] A time to love, and a time to hate; a time of war, and a time of peace.

5. **Luke 21:19 KJV**
    [19] In your patience possess ye your souls.

6. **Psalm 46:1-3 KJV**
    [1] God is our refuge and strength, a very present help in trouble. [2] Therefore will not we fear, though the earth be removed, and though the mountains be carried into the midst of the sea; [3] Though the waters thereof roar and be troubled, though the mountains shake with the swelling thereof. Selah.

7. **Hebrews 11:1 KJV**
    [1] Now faith is the substance of things hoped for, the evidence of things not seen.

8. **Genesis 2:15-17 KJV**
    [15] And the Lord God took the man, and put him into the garden of Eden to dress it and to keep it. [16] And the Lord God commanded the man, saying, Of every tree of the garden thou mayest freely eat: [17] But of the tree of the knowledge of good and evil, thou shalt not eat of it: for in the day that thou eatest thereof thou shalt surely die.

9. **Matthew 1:1-17 KJV**
    [1] The book of the generation of Jesus Christ, the son of David, the son of Abraham. [2] Abraham begat Isaac; and Isaac begat Jacob; and Jacob begat Judas and his brethren; [3] And Judas begat Phares and Zara of Thamar; and Phares begat Esrom; and Esrom begat Aram; [4] And Aram begat Aminadab; and Aminadab begat Naasson; and Naasson begat

Salmon; [5] And Salmon begat Booz of Rachab; and Booz begat Obed of Ruth; and Obed begat Jesse; [6] And Jesse begat David the king; and David the king begat Solomon of her that had been the wife of Urias; [7] And Solomon begat Roboam; and Roboam begat Abia; and Abia begat Asa; [8] And Asa begat Josaphat; and Josaphat begat Joram; and Joram begat Ozias; [9] And Ozias begat Joatham; and Joatham begat Achaz; and Achaz begat Ezekias; [10] And Ezekias begat Manasses; and Manasses begat Amon; and Amon begat Josias; [11] And Josias begat Jechonias and his brethren, about the time they were carried away to Babylon: [12] And after they were brought to Babylon, Jechonias begat Salathiel; and Salathiel begat Zorobabel; [13] And Zorobabel begat Abiud; and Abiud begat Eliakim; and Eliakim begat Azor; [14] And Azor begat Sadoc; and Sadoc begat Achim; and Achim begat Eliud; [15] And Eliud begat Eleazar; and Eleazar begat Matthan; and Matthan begat Jacob; [16] And Jacob begat Joseph the husband of Mary, of whom was born Jesus, who is called Christ. [17] So all the generations from Abraham to David are fourteen generations; and from David until the carrying away into Babylon are fourteen generations; and from the carrying away into Babylon unto Christ are fourteen generations.

10. Jeremiah 29:11 KJV

[11] For I know the thoughts that I think toward you, saith the Lord, thoughts of peace, and not of evil, to give you an expected end.

11. Proverbs 4:20-23 KJV

[20] My son, attend to my words; incline thine ear unto my sayings. [21] Let them not depart from thine eyes; keep them in the midst of thine heart. [22] For

they are life unto those that find them, and health to all their flesh. [23] Keep thy heart with all diligence; for out of it are the issues of life.

12. **Jeremiah 17:9 KJV**
[9] The heart is deceitful above all things, and desperately wicked: who can know it?

13. **1 Samuel 1:1-5 KJV**
[1] Now there was a certain man of Ramathaim-zophim, of mount Ephraim, and his name was Elkanah, the son of Jeroham, the son of Elihu, the son of Tohu, the son of Zuph, an Ephrathite: [2] And he had two wives; the name of the one was Hannah, and the name of the other Peninnah: and Peninnah had children, but Hannah had no children. [3] And this man went up out of his city yearly to worship and to sacrifice unto the Lord of hosts in Shiloh. And the two sons of Eli, Hophni and Phinehas, the priests of the Lord, were there. [4] And when the time was that Elkanah offered, he gave to Peninnah his wife, and to all her sons and her daughters, portions: [5] But unto Hannah he gave a worthy portion; for he loved Hannah: but the Lord had shut up her womb.

14. **Psalm 119:67-72 KJV**
[67] Before I was afflicted I went astray: but now have I kept thy word. [68] Thou art good, and doest good; teach me thy statutes. [69] The proud have forged a lie against me: but I will keep thy precepts with my whole heart. [70] Their heart is as fat as grease; but I delight in thy law. [71] It is good for me that I have been afflicted; that I might learn thy statutes. [72] The law of thy mouth is better unto me than thousands of gold and silver.

15. 2 Corinthians 12:7-10 KJV

[7] And lest I should be exalted above measure through the abundance of the revelations, there was given to me a thorn in the flesh, the messenger of Satan to buffet me, lest I should be exalted above measure. [8] For this thing I besought the Lord thrice, that it might depart from me. [9] And he said unto me, My grace is sufficient for thee: for my strength is made perfect in weakness. Most gladly therefore will I rather glory in my infirmities, that the power of Christ may rest upon me. [10] Therefore I take pleasure in infirmities, in reproaches, in necessities, in persecutions, in distresses for Christ's sake: for when I am weak, then am I strong.

16. Matthew 7:12 KJV

[12] Therefore all things whatsoever ye would that men should do to you, do ye even so to them: for this is the law and the prophets.

17. Psalm 150:1-6 KJV

[1] Praise ye the Lord. Praise God in his sanctuary: praise him in the firmament of his power. [2] Praise him for his mighty acts: praise him according to his excellent greatness. [3] Praise him with the sound of the trumpet: praise him with the psaltery and harp. [4] Praise him with the timbrel and dance: praise him with stringed instruments and organs. [5] Praise him upon the loud cymbals: praise him upon the high sounding cymbals. [6] Let every thing that hath breath praise the Lord. Praise ye the Lord.

18. Ezekiel 28:11-14 KJV

[11] Moreover the word of the Lord came unto me, saying, [12] Son of man, take up a lamentation upon

the king of Tyrus, and say unto him, Thus saith the Lord God; Thou sealest up the sum, full of wisdom, and perfect in beauty. [13] Thou hast been in Eden the garden of God; every precious stone was thy covering, the sardius, topaz, and the diamond, the beryl, the onyx, and the jasper, the sapphire, the emerald, and the carbuncle, and gold: the workmanship of thy tabrets and of thy pipes was prepared in thee in the day that thou wast created. [14] Thou art the anointed cherub that covereth; and I have set thee so: thou wast upon the holy mountain of God; thou hast walked up and down in the midst of the stones of fire.

19. Psalm 22:1-4 KJV

[1] My God, my God, why hast thou forsaken me? why art thou so far from helping me, and from the words of my roaring? [2] O my God, I cry in the daytime, but thou hearest not; and in the night season, and am not silent. [3] But thou art holy, O thou that inhabitest the praises of Israel. [4] Our fathers trusted in thee: they trusted, and thou didst deliver them.

20. 2 Samuel 6:15-23 KJV

[15] So David and all the house of Israel brought up the ark of the Lord with shouting, and with the sound of the trumpet. [16] And as the ark of the Lord came into the city of David, Michal Saul's daughter looked through a window, and saw king David leaping and dancing before the Lord; and she despised him in her heart. [17] And they brought in the ark of the Lord, and set it in his place, in the midst of the tabernacle that David had pitched for it: and David offered burnt offerings and peace offerings before the Lord. [18] And as soon as David had made an end of

offering burnt offerings and peace offerings, he blessed the people in the name of the Lord of hosts. [19] And he dealt among all the people, even among the whole multitude of Israel, as well to the women as men, to every one a cake of bread, and a good piece of flesh, and a flagon of wine. So all the people departed every one to his house. [20] Then David returned to bless his household. And Michal the daughter of Saul came out to meet David, and said, How glorious was the king of Israel to day, who uncovered himself to day in the eyes of the handmaids of his servants, as one of the vain fellows shamelessly uncovereth himself! [21] And David said unto Michal, It was before the Lord, which chose me before thy father, and before all his house, to appoint me ruler over the people of the Lord, over Israel: therefore will I play before the Lord. [22] And I will yet be more vile than thus, and will be base in mine own sight: and of the maidservants which thou hast spoken of, of them shall I be had in honour. [23] Therefore Michal the daughter of Saul had no child unto the day of her death.

21. Luke 12:34 KJV

[34] For where your treasure is, there will your heart be also.

22. Matthew 6:31-34 KJV

[31] Therefore take no thought, saying, What shall we eat? or, What shall we drink? or, Wherewithal shall we be clothed? [32] (For after all these things do the Gentiles seek:) for your heavenly Father knoweth that ye have need of all these things. [33] But seek ye first the kingdom of God, and his righteousness; and all these things shall be added unto you. [34] Take therefore no thought for the

morrow: for the morrow shall take thought for the things of itself. Sufficient unto the day is the evil thereof.

23. **John 5:1-9 KJV**
[1] After this there was a feast of the Jews; and Jesus went up to Jerusalem. [2] Now there is at Jerusalem by the sheep market a pool, which is called in the Hebrew tongue Bethesda, having five porches. [3] In these lay a great multitude of impotent folk, of blind, halt, withered, waiting for the moving of the water. [4] For an angel went down at a certain season into the pool, and troubled the water: whosoever then first after the troubling of the water stepped in was made whole of whatsoever disease he had. [5] And a certain man was there, which had an infirmity thirty and eight years. [6] When Jesus saw him lie, and knew that he had been now a long time in that case, he saith unto him, Wilt thou be made whole? [7] The impotent man answered him, Sir, I have no man, when the water is troubled, to put me into the pool: but while I am coming, another steppeth down before me. [8] Jesus saith unto him, Rise, take up thy bed, and walk. [9] And immediately the man was made whole, and took up his bed, and walked: and on the same day was the sabbath.

24. **Proverbs 23:7 KJV**
[7] For as he thinketh in his heart, so is he: Eat and drink, saith he to thee; but his heart is not with thee.

25. **Philippians 2:1-8 KJV**
[1] If there be therefore any consolation in Christ, if any comfort of love, if any fellowship of the Spirit, if any bowels and mercies, [2] Fulfil ye my joy, that ye be likeminded, having the same love, being of one

accord, of one mind. [3] Let nothing be done through strife or vainglory; but in lowliness of mind let each esteem other better than themselves. [4] Look not every man on his own things, but every man also on the things of others. [5] Let this mind be in you, which was also in Christ Jesus: [6] Who, being in the form of God, thought it not robbery to be equal with God: [7] But made himself of no reputation, and took upon him the form of a servant, and was made in the likeness of men: [8] And being found in fashion as a man, he humbled himself, and became obedient unto death, even the death of the cross.

26. Matthew 23:11-12 KJV

[11] But he that is greatest among you shall be your servant. [12] And whosoever shall exalt himself shall be abased; and he that shall humble himself shall be exalted.

27. 2 Chronicles 26:1-4,14-16 KJV

[1] Then all the people of Judah took Uzziah, who was sixteen years old, and made him king in the room of his father Amaziah. [2] He built Eloth, and restored it to Judah, after that the king slept with his fathers. [3] Sixteen years old was Uzziah when he began to reign, and he reigned fifty and two years in Jerusalem. His mother's name also was Jecoliah of Jerusalem. [4] And he did that which was right in the sight of the Lord, according to all that his father Amaziah did. [14] And Uzziah prepared for them throughout all the host shields, and spears, and helmets, and habergeons, and bows, and slings to cast stones. [15] And he made in Jerusalem engines, invented by cunning men, to be on the towers and upon the bulwarks, to shoot arrows and great stones withal. And his name spread far abroad; for he was

marvellously helped, till he was strong. [16] But when he was strong, his heart was lifted up to his destruction: for he transgressed against the Lord his God, and went into the temple of the Lord to burn incense upon the altar of incense.

28. 1 Corinthians 12:4-12 KJV

[4] Now there are diversities of gifts, but the same Spirit. [5] And there are differences of administrations, but the same Lord. [6] And there are diversities of operations, but it is the same God which worketh all in all. [7] But the manifestation of the Spirit is given to every man to profit withal. [8] For to one is given by the Spirit the word of wisdom; to another the word of knowledge by the same Spirit; [9] To another faith by the same Spirit; to another the gifts of healing by the same Spirit; [10] To another the working of miracles; to another prophecy; to another discerning of spirits; to another divers kinds of tongues; to another the interpretation of tongues: [11] But all these worketh that one and the selfsame Spirit, dividing to every man severally as he will. [12] For as the body is one, and hath many members, and all the members of that one body, being many, are one body: so also is Christ.

Made in the USA
Lexington, KY
27 August 2017